London's 'Disgraceful Vardapet':

Armenian priest, Adulterer, Soviet Agent

Felix Corley, Philippe Sukiasyan, Jakub Osiecki

 կ

Gomidas Institute
London

Felix Corley is the author of *Catholicos and Commissar: The Armenian Church Under the Soviet Regime* (Gomidas Institute, London, 2025).

Philippe Sukiasyan is co-author of the chapter L'Église dans l'Arménie contemporaine (1921-2007) in *Histoire du peuple arménien* (Éditions Privat, Toulouse, 2007).

Jakub Osiecki is the author of *The Armenian Church in Soviet Armenia: The Policies of the Armenian Bolsheviks and the Armenian Church 1920-1932* (Peter Lang, New York, 2020).

ISBN 978-1-909382-89-3

Gomidas Institute
42 Blythe Rd.
London W14 0HA
England
www.gomidas.org
info@gomidas.org

CONTENTS

Introduction

Abel Abrahamian arrived in London in 1919 as a dashing young vardapet (celibate priest), multi-lingual, well educated, handsome and energetic. He was instrumental in the building of the city's first Armenian church, St Sarkis, and bringing in the oil magnate Calouste Gulbenkian to bankroll the project. As with his earlier time in Germany as a student, the young priest forged close friendships with members of other Christian communities, not just the nuns in the North London convent where he regularly held services before St Sarkis was built but with leading figures in the Church of England and internationally. He was received by the Archbishop of Canterbury and joined him and the Patriarch of Constantinople when they were received by the king at Buckingham Palace. At a time when the plight of Armenia and the Armenians was of wide public concern following the genocide, he spoke forcefully and eloquently from public platforms, rubbing shoulders with prominent politicians and public figures. He even spoke at one London event when Armenia's General Antranig had to remain silent for lack of time. A growing list of publications in various languages flowed from his pen. The young vardapet, by now going by the name Nazarian, was a rising star in the Church.

Yet all this came to an abrupt and undignified halt, when in 1923 he fled London with a young wife and mother, a close relative of Calouste Gulbenkian. The handsome vardapet was now an adulterer, leaving division and confusion in the church and bitterness in the Gulbenkian family. Calouste Gulbenkian ensured that the former priest's name was erased from the ceremonial plaque on the church the two had worked together to build. Even more extraordinary, the vardapet who had abandoned his holy orders then teamed up with the Cheka, the Soviet secret police, to help destroy the Church which had trained and nurtured him. He returned to Armenia – by now Sovietised – and spoke and wrote against his erstwhile colleagues. But here too he failed to settle. Within a year he had managed to extricate himself and was now in France with a wife and young daughter (with a son soon to follow), where – after a sort of apology to the Armenian Catholicos – he largely disappeared from public view.

How a young man born on the southern rim of the then Russian Empire, educated at Echmiadzin seminary and the universities of Marburg and Zurich, came and went in a whirlwind through London and Manchester and back to Soviet Armenia before regaining western Europe is the extraordinary tale told here from surviving documents for the first time.[*]

Seminary, Ordination

According to his diploma on completing studies at Echmiadzin[†] and information he later submitted for his university studies in Europe, Abel Abrahamian was born on 1 April 1888 into an Armenian family in Dashburun (a Turkic place name meaning Stone Nose), in Surmali *uezd* of Yerevan *guberniya* of the Russian Empire, 8 kms (5 miles) south of the river Arax and close to the town of Igdir (now in Turkey). The village had a population of 2,126, of whom 2,103 were listed as 'Armenian Gregorians', according to the Tsarist 1897 census. The village had a church and a primary school. Whether Abel was his given name as well as his priestly name remains unknown.

Information provided by his son at his death in 1965 gives Abel's parents' names as Serop Nazarian and Soussane Gregorian. If Abel's father's surname was indeed Nazarian, it remains unclear why Abel initially had the surname Abrahamian. His son declared that Abel had

* The authors are grateful to the archivists at the Armenian National Archive in Yerevan, Lambeth Palace in London and the World Council of Churches in Geneva. They also thank Dr Jonathan Conlin of the University of Southampton, Dr Katharina Schaal of Philipps-Universität Marburg, the staff of Holy Translators Cathedral in Marseille, Fr Jirayr Tashjian and Jean-Pierre Hatchikian at the Armenian church library in Paris, and Gagik Stepan-Sarkissian of the Armenian Institute in London.
† Armenian National Archive (ANA), Yerevan, f. 312, op. 2, d. 17, p. 2.

been born in Salmas, Iran, on 14 April 1890.* Whether his son had misread 'Surmali' on an old document as 'Salmas' and why he gave his date of birth as two years later than it was (taking account of Old and New Style dates) remain unclear. Possibly Abel deliberately changed his date and place of birth to avoid any enforced repatriation to the Soviet Union, as many who fled the Soviet Union did.

Presumably it was his parents who sent the young Abel to study at the junior seminary at Echmiadzin, where he arrived in 1901 aged 13. It is difficult to tell if his later account of why boys at that time were sent to the seminary – although couched in general terms it seems likely he was speaking also of himself – was a retrospective reinterpretation.

> Armenian parents working in agriculture had a great desire to entrust their children to the Academy, mainly because the education was free while we know that during the period of the Tsarist ancien régime, only the rich were in a position to enrol their children in the most prestigious schools. This situation, that is the modest circumstances of Academy students of rural origin, allowed the leaders of the Academy to behave in a way that was different to what one has the right to expect from heads of a scholarly institution.

Abel does not appear to have given any insight into any personal vocation, noting that

> we all consider the Armenian Church the national institution called to deliver this or that type of service as part of Armenian society. I am fully convinced that none of us was animated by religious sentiments at the moment he decided to enter religion. We did not decide to enter religion for the salvation of our own souls or to save those of others.†

Abel appears to have been a promising student, as his first year marks for the 1900-1 school year were either the top grade 5, or a 4. On 16

---

* Death certificate No. 203, 3 October 1965, Mairie du Raincy.
† *Why I Left*, pp. 3 and 7.

April 1907, when he had just turned 19, the seminary's pedagogical council confirmed he had completed his studies. Noting his conduct as excellent, it gave him generally good grades, including in Scripture, church singing, church history, ancient Armenian history and geography, general history and geography, and arithmetic. His knowledge of Russian and German, as well as of algebra and geography of Russia were noted as satisfactory. The seminary rector Vardapet Mesrop signed the certificate on 16 May.[*]

Abrahamian was then accepted into higher studies. Two years later, by agreement with Gurgen Edilian, the professor of pedagogy, he proposed as the subject of his study the German philosopher and pioneering educationalist Johann Friedrich Herbart (1776-1841).[†] His choice of study topic appears to indicate that he had by now a reasonable command of German. His study was published in Tiflis in 1911, with a translation of Herbart's work *Psychology and Logic* published in Echmiadzin two years later.

After gaining his diploma in June 1910, Abrahamian was approved for ordination as a celibate priest at the age of 23 in 1911, becoming a member of the Echmiadzin brotherhood. The Church's journal *Ararat* recorded the decision: 'On 16 March, No. 191, the Synod, having heard the kondak of His Holiness, the deceased Catholicos, of 21 October, No. 2272, decided to accept Abel Abraham, a resident of Dashburun, into the spiritual vocation, as a monk of the Mother See, in accordance with his case.'[‡]

That same year Abrahamian became a member of the organising committee for the blessing of *myron* (chrism) ceremony at Echmiadzin where, by his later account, he was in charge of handling the 'multitudes' of pilgrims who came from Armenia and further

---

[*] ANA, f. 312, op. 2, d. 17, p. 31.

[†] ANA, f. 312, op. 2, d. 17, pp. 2ff (Abrahamian's written proposal to study Herbart).

[‡] *Ararat*, April 1911, p. 271.

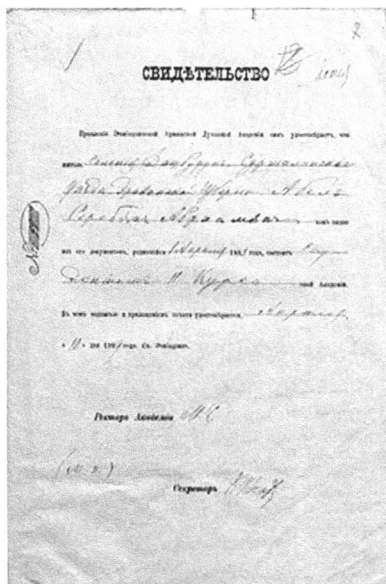

afield. In 1911-2, he also served as editor of the church journal *Ararat*, alongside the linguist Manuk Abegyan.[*] By 1913, he was already listed among brotherhood members as a vardapet.[†] The Caucasian Calendar for 1913, published in 1912, lists a 'Vardapet Abel' as the Armenian history teacher at Echmiadzin seminary.[‡]

European Studies

As with other gifted graduates of the seminary, the young Fr Abrahamian was earmarked for further study in Germany, the chosen destination for many of the Church's most promising clerics.

---

[*] Information from a 1931 list compiled by Bishop Artak Smbatyan. *Արտակ եպիսկոպոս Սմբատեանց (Տաուշեցի): Հոգևոր, գրական, պատմաբանասիրական գործունեությունը ընդակահարությունը (1876-1937թթ.)* (Bishop Artak Smbatyants (Taushetsi): Spiritual, Literary, Historical and Philological Activities and Execution (1876-1937)), (Anahit, Yerevan, 1997), p. 509.

[†] *Մ. Կերտող, ՀԱՅ ԱՌԱՔԵԼԱԿԱՆ ԵԿԵՂԵՑԻՆ ԱՌԱՋԻՆ ԱՇԽԱՐՀԱՄԱՐՏԻ ՏԱՐԻՆԵՐԻՆ* (History of the Armenian Apostolic Church in the First World War), Echmiadzin, 2003, p. 16.

[‡] *Kavkazsky kalendar na 1913 god* (Tiflis, 1912), column 619.

Announcements were placed in several Caucasian newspapers for the second time in 1911 offering scholarships for Armenian Apostolic applicants to study in a wide range of subjects in Russian or European universities in a programme initiated by the Armenian oil magnate and benefactor, Alexander Mantashev. A separate announcement was made for religious applicants, funded by the estate of the businessman Avetis Lukasian.

> The administration of the Gevorgian Theological Academy announces that the interest on the sum bequeathed by A. Lukasian will be used to send either a clergyman of the Armenian Apostolic Church (vardapet, priest, celibate clergyman) or someone who agrees to enter the clergy and serve the Armenian Church in the Caucasus, Turkey, or Persia, to study theology abroad. a) Applicants must be graduates of the Gevorgian Academy. b) A certified copy of the diploma must be enclosed with the application. c) The Academy's Pedagogical Council will give preference to studies in theology, history, philology, literature, music, or canon law. d) The scholarship is 800 roubles per year. All applications received by February of the following year, 1913, will be considered.

Two applicants applied, of whom only Abrahamian was accepted. He had applied to study canon law in Germany or history in England. He stressed in his application that he knew enough German to be able to begin studies with no difficulty. But he added that as 'so many students from Echmiadzin go to study in Germany', he was ready to go to England to study history. The pedagogical council believed that studying canon law, especially in a country where it was taught 'at a very high level', was more important. It sent him to Germany with an annual grant of 800 roubles. He pledged to repay the grant if, after completing his studies, he chose to withdraw from the priesthood or did anything that caused Echmiadzin to defrock him.[*]

Abrahamian was in his mid-twenties when on 27 October 1913 he enrolled in the law faculty of Marburg University, where he would study for two semesters. The small town of about 25,000 people in the province of Hesse-Nassau, with its medieval university, was a leading academic centre. On matriculation, Abrahamian gave his father's profession as farmer, indicating that he still lived in Dashburun. On re-enrolling the following semester, he gave his religion as 'Armenian Gregorian' and his father's occupation this time as merchant.[†] He presented a letter from Echmiadzin to the university administration to prove his financial state.

> The administration of the theological academy of Echmiadzin hereby confirms that Abel Abrahamian, a hiero-monk from Dashburun in Russian Armenia, is the recipient of a grant from our academy, under which he receives 800 roubles each year. In confirmation of this is this declaration with the seal of the academy and with the signature of the rector.[‡]

But financial worries marked Abrahamian's student years, both in Germany and later in Switzerland. He wrote from Marburg to the academy leadership in Echmiadzin lamenting that after paying his student fees, rent, clothing, as well as German lessons (2 Marks an hour), he had no money left for anything else. He asked for the grant for the next half year to be sent early. A later letter asked the academy in Echmiadzin for urgent support, declaring that 'the respected

---

[*] ANA, f. 312, op. 1, d. 55. Arpine Maniero, *Umkämpfter Weg zur Bildung: Armenische Studierende in Deutschland und der Schweiz von der Mitte des 19. bis Anfang des 20. Jahrhunderts* (Vandenhoeck & Ruprecht, Göttingen, 2020), pp. 242-3.

[†] *Matrikelband vom Wintersemester 1913/4*, UniA Marburg 305m 1 Nr. 59; *Matrikelband vom Sommersemester 1914*, UniA Marburg 305m 1 Nr. 60. These give his date and place of birth, as do his Zurich University records.

[‡] ANA, f. 312, op. 1, d. 55, p. 244. Maniero, p. 243.

administration should definitely be in the picture as to what it means to live in Germany with no money, above all in a town with no Armenians'. An extra cost in Marburg flowed from the requirement that law students know Latin. He repeatedly asked Echmiadzin for funds to pay the costs of his Latin studies. When money arrived, Abrahamian believed his appeal had been successful, only to be disappointed when it transpired that the payment was his regular grant.[*]

In Marburg the young cleric became a close friend of and frequent guest at the home of the Protestant theologian Martin Rade, professor of Evangelical theology at the university. But as a subject of the Russian Empire, a country at war with Germany, life for the young priest became increasingly difficult, even though in December 1915 the German culture minister would authorise Armenian students to continue their studies. But in early 1915, Abrahamian had already decided to transfer to the university of Zurich in neutral Switzerland. He left Marburg with some misgivings, particularly missing the warm hospitality of the Rade household, as he wrote to the professor on 14 March 1915.[†]

Abrahamian enrolled in the faculty of public law at Zurich University, living in rented accommodation in Turnerstrasse, an elegant street of four or five storey houses. He was not the first Echmiadzin graduate to have studied at the university. Aram Akulian, originally from Alexandropol in northern Armenia, had studied history and chemistry there, graduating four years before Abrahamian arrived. And arriving the same year as Abrahamian to study philosophy was another Echmiadzin graduate, Hakob Haroutiunian. Originally from Tabriz and a Persian subject, he would graduate in 1916. In addition, a native of Vardablur, Lori, Harutyun Abelyants,

---

[*] ANA, f. 312, op. 1, d. 55, pp. 251-4. Maniero, pp. 243-4.

[†] Axel Meißner, *Martin Rades "Christliche Welt" und Armenien: Bausteine für eine internationale Ethik des Protestantismus* (LIT Verlag, Münster, 2010), pp. 222, 429. Martin Rade's Archive at Marburg University contains the 1915 letter from Abrahamian to Rade and the signed copy of his published thesis.

was a long-established professor there.[*] The future bishop Arsen Ghlutchian also studied at Zurich University from 1907, graduating in 1911.[†]

As genocide raged in the Ottoman Empire, Abrahamian took time out from his studies to participate in various public events. In September 1916, he and Professor Abelyants were among the participants in a conference in the Swiss city of Basel, together with Johannes Lepsius, a German long sympathetic to the plight of the Armenians, to raise awareness and funds for Armenians in the Ottoman Empire and to discuss what political future there could be for Armenian self-determination.

Financial worries had followed Abrahamian from Marburg to Zurich, worsened by the rouble's exchange rate during the First World War. He gave the Holy Synod in Echmiadzin a vivid picture of his plight.

> In order that the respected administration gains an understanding of how I am living since my move to Zurich, I will mention only that I eat in a canteen for the poor for 70 centimes at lunchtime and 50 centimes for an evening meal. For almost a year I have been unable to buy new clothes, while the cheapest shoes that one can get cost 25 francs. Without wanting to dwell too much, I would just like to draw the attention of the Holy Synod to the fact that my sole concern is for my health, which I have no intention of leaving in Switzerland.

Despite his financial woes, Abrahamian was a diligent student, studying Catholic canon law and learning Latin. By 1917 he had completed his German-language dissertation, entitled *Die Grundlagen des armenischen Kirchenrechts* (The Bases of Armenian

---

* Information on Abrahamian's studies at Zurich University from the university matriculation records at https://www.matrikel.uzh.ch/active/static/659.htm.
† https://www.matrikel.uzh.ch/active/static/11685.htm, where his name is spelled Arsen Klidschian.

Canon Law). The work was based on reading in a range of languages: the bibliography cites 17 works in German, 12 in French, 10 in Armenian and 3 in Russian. He asked the Echmiadzin academy's pedagogical council for 400 francs for the exam costs and 100 francs to cover the cost of typing the work twice. No response arrived from Echmiadzin, so he had to borrow the money to make the deadline. This left him no money – after paying his rent of 150 francs – even for cigarettes and matches. Covering the 920 franc cost of printing the dissertation – a university requirement – was a struggle: the printing company would not hand over the copies until he had paid. He feared having to hold off lodging the dissertation for another year.* How he found the money to pay for the printing remains unclear.

Abrahamian formally left the university on 12 May 1917 after completing exams and graduating. The same year he published his dissertation as a 163-page book, printed by the local dissertation printing company Leemann and Co. On the cover he is billed as 'Doctor of Law, A. Abrahamian, member of the cathedral monastery of Holy Echmiadzin'. Abrahamian was clearly proud of his handiwork, which he was eager to present to his academic friends. He autographed a copy with a dedication on 21 August 1917 for Professor Rade back in Marburg.

German pastor Ewald Stier, from the Anhalt Lutheran Church, a supporter of Armenians who had visited the Caucasus, appears to have been impressed by Abrahamian's study and pastoral work.

> Many of the [Armenian] higher clergy have also been sent by the Church to Russian or (since 1891) German universities, where they not only follow theological but also philosophical, and a few also musical studies. Recently an Armenian archimandrite has even studied law in Germany and Switzerland in order to be able to serve his Church in

---

* ANA, f. 312, op. 1, d. 55, pp. 354, 369. Maniero, p. 244.

its wide-ranging administrative activities. He received his doctorate in law in Zurich and has given us a worthwhile work on the bases of Armenian canon law. At the same time he currently holds the post of pastor in the Armenian community in Marseille, following his additional church service during his studies for the numerous Armenians in Geneva.[*]

At Christmas 1917, Abrahamian travelled to Geneva to hold a Christmas service in the Christian Catholic (Old Catholic) Church of Saint-Germain in the city, as an Ottoman official reported back to his government.[†] In 1917-18, Abrahamian served briefly in the Armenian church in Marseille in the south of France. He was the sixth, though temporary, priest of St Haroutiun's chapel, then housed in a block of flats in rue St Jacques near the port.[‡]

Ministry in London

By early 1919 Vardapet Abrahamian was already in London, describing himself as Right Reverend Dr Abel Abrahamian and as 'suffragan bishop' for Britain's Armenian community. In addition to his pastoral, community and public work, he was soon ensconcing himself in the heart of the British establishment. In a letter to Echmiadzin written in late 1920, Abrahamian explained his intention in having taken the London job:

> In March 1919 I received a letter from the London Armenian Council inviting me to become the local pastor. Although I did not wish to be tied down by a new position

[*] Ewald Stier, 'Die Armenische Kirche', *Mitteilungen über Armenien* (Basel), No. 7, 1918, p. 69. Maniero, pp. 246-7.
[†] State Archives of the Prime Ministry, Ankara, Turkey, HR.SYS 2884/22 Belge No: 1, http://www.devletarsivleri.gov.tr/icerik/1180/cenevredeki-ermenilerin-noel-dolayisiyla-saint-germain-kilisesinde-papaz-abel-abrahamian-in-katili/.
[‡] Information from Secretariat of Holy Translators Cathedral, Marseille, 10 January 2017; and from Stephan Boghossian, Marseille, 3 February 2017.

in any place until my return to Holy Echmiadzin, as I had rejected a similar request from America, one issue compelled me to accept the pastorate in London: the issue of establishing an Armenian church in London. That's the reason I accepted that position and I have been doing it for a year and a half now.

One of Abrahamian's first actions was to call a meeting that May to plan for building the proposed new London church, which he chaired. He also expressed an interest in further studies in Oxford, as he wrote to Catholicos Gevorg V, though nothing appears to have come of this:

> By being in Oxford I would not only get closely acquainted with Anglican theological knowledge, but would have an opportunity to establish connections with major figures in the field of Anglican education, church and politics, which would certainly have major benefits for my activities as a clergyman.[*]

On 19 June 1919, soon after his arrival in London, Abrahamian was on stage at Westminster's Central Hall for a high profile public meeting on 'Armenia and the Settlement', which aimed to 'express sympathy with the Armenian cause'. Chaired by Viscount Gladstone, son of the prime minister and himself a former home secretary, the meeting hosted a thronged stage of key speakers which also included Viscount Bryce – the co-compiler of *The Treatment of Armenians in the Ottoman Empire* – and from Armenia General Antranig Ozanian. Abrahamian spoke – in French – as the last main speaker at the end of what must have been a long evening. He greeted the meeting 'as pastor of the Armenians in London' and expressed his gratitude 'in the name of his compatriots'. He spoke of Armenia's ancient Christian Church and claimed the country's culture 'became for centuries the vanguard of western civilisation in the East'. He noted

---

[*] Quoted in *On the Occasion of...*, p. 12.

12

that Armenia – 'massacred, martyred' – was then 'emerging from the blood of her heroes, from the ashes of her martyrs, and the tears of their survivors'. Antranig – despite being received 'with unbounded enthusiasm' – was among those not given the chance to speak because of the 'lateness of the hour' as the meeting concluded. Anyone who wished to know what the general had intended to say had to wait until the publication of the speeches from the evening in a booklet issued by the Armenian Bureau in London that year. Abrahamian's name proudly figures among the 13 key speakers listed on the front cover. [*]

In November 1919, Abrahamian was one of those who welcomed Avetis Aharonian, who headed the Armenian national delegation to the Paris peace conference, to a meeting of the Armenian United Association of London at their offices at 47a Redcliffe Square in Chelsea. Eight days later, at the same offices, he helped welcome Boghos Nubar Pasha, the other head of the Armenian delegation to

---

[*] An account of the meeting is also in *Ararat: A Searchlight on Armenia* (London), Summer 1919, pp. 413-5. The same issue contains a summary of Abrahamian's thesis on Armenian canon law, pp. 433-43.

the peace conference.[*] Also in that November, Abrahamian was a leading member of the Armenian delegation which went to Buckingham Palace to greet the visiting Shah of Persia. Among the other delegates was Nerses Gulbenkian, a London merchant who was a cousin of the oil magnate Calouste Gulbenkian.[†]

Abrahamian was also involved in the fledgling British Armenian Chamber of Commerce in London. The minutes of the 26 November 1919 meeting of its Council record his presence as 'Bishop of Armenia' and his contribution to discussions.

> Today the war was over and the Peace Conference had settled the affairs of the world...

> He was of the opinion that the best method of helping Armenia which the British Armenian Chamber of Commerce could adopt would be to advocate the recognition, at least provisionally, of the present Armenian Republic of Erivan to which had been added as many as 400,000 refugees from Turkish Armenia, that was the nucleus of the nation.

Abrahamian does not appear to have played much of a further role in the Chamber of Commerce. The minutes of the 3 March 1920 meeting – attended by invitation by the visiting Boghos Nubar Pasha and Patriarch Zaven Der Yeghiayan of Constantinople – record that Abrahamian was not present.[‡]

In January 1920, Abrahamian presided over and spoke at a number of events in and around Manchester – where the Armenian church was well established – to support Armenian orphans. At an event organised by the Manchester Armenian Ladies' Guild, '£600 was

---

[*] *Ararat*, November/December 1919, pp. 530-4.
[†] *The Times*, 13 November 1919, p. 7. *Ararat*, November/December 1919, pp. 537-8.
[‡] The minute book is in London Metropolitan Archives, CLC/B/150/MS16510.

Bishop. Abel Abrahamian

collected, and when the Bishop made an eloquent appeal for the adoption of orphans, the response resulted in the adoption of no less than one hundred'. An event organised by 'the Armenian ladies of Southport' brought in nearly £7,000 'on the spot' after he and another speaker 'made stirring appeals to the national sentiment of their hearers'.[*]

By now, the London priest was completing work on what would be published as *The Church and Faith of Armenia* by the London publisher The Faith Press in 1920. Rev. John Douglas, an Anglican vicar in Camberwell and a keen ecumenist who was particularly interested in and sympathetic towards the Eastern Churches, appears to have been closely involved in encouraging and promoting – perhaps even commissioning – Abrahamian to produce the work. Douglas – the co-founder with his brother of the Society of Faith, which appears to have sponsored the work for its publishing house – may too have polished the English text. 'The Armenian Bishop in London has just written me a short popular book on the Armenian Church,' Douglas

[*] *Ararat*, 1920, p. 18.

wrote to Rev. Professor H. J. White of the Church of England's Eastern Churches Committee on 16 January 1920. 'I wonder whether you could get the Bishop of Gibraltar or the Bishop of Gloucester to write a preface, preferably the former whom I do not know.' Douglas offered to send White the typeset proofs of the book as soon as he had them.[*]

In the book as published later that year, the author was billed as 'The Rt. Rev. Dr. Abel Abrahamian, Supreme Vardapet of Armenians in England, author of *Die Grundlagen des armenischen Kirchenrechts*, Zurich, 1917'. A portrait of the author sitting in simple clerical dress in a wooden armchair clutching an open book graced the frontispiece, with a note describing him as 'The Armenian Vardapet who exercises episcopal jurisdiction in England'. Among the other illustrations in the book was one of Abrahamian 'fully vested'. The author's cultivation of the Anglicans paid off with a preface by Edgar Gibson, Bishop of Gloucester, who noted that the volume 'enables English readers to see exactly what the Armenians say of themselves; for it is actually written by an Armenian Vardapet'.

The 75-page book gives a straightforward, readable account of the nation and the Church. But Abrahamian used the opportunity to set out what he saw as the need to resolve 'the problem of reformation in the Armenian Church'.

> That the Armenian Church is in need of reform is obvious; that some of its rites and ceremonies, which have been kept unchanged for centuries, do not respond to modern requirements, every one knows; that the standard of education for the Armenian clergy should be raised, is the desire of every Armenian, and that all Armenian prelates

---

[*] Lambeth Palace Library, MS 3909, p. 16.

THE CHURCH AND
FAITH OF ARMENIA

By
THE RT. REV. DR. ABEL ABRAHAMIAN
Supreme Vardapet of Armenians in England; Author of
Die Grundlagen des Armenischen Kirchenrechts (Zürich F, 1917)

LONDON
THE FAITH PRESS
22 BUCKINGHAM STREET, CHARING CROSS, W.C.2
1920

The Very Rev. Dr. Abel Abrahamian,
The Armenian Vardapet who exercises episcopal jurisdiction
in England.

have realised the deficiencies of their Church is evident from the fact that, whenever favourable conditions have been secured, the Armenian Catholicos has secured reform.

Abrahamian insisted though that such reform 'must be based on different principles from those advocated by our Protestant and Catholic friends'. He criticised Protestants who were urging the use of modern Armenian in the liturgy immediately and maintained that, 'while realising the need of a fresh translation of the Bible' the Armenian Church was obliged to wait until spoken Armenian in the western and eastern parts of the region became more standardised out of a desire not to cause 'injury to the unity of the Church'. Abrahamian – who completed his book in early 1920 – welcomed what he saw as the advantage Catholicos Gevorg V took in calling a church synod to discuss reforms in summer 1917, 'immediately after the Russian Revolution, before the advent of Bolshevism'. In discussing a new Church constitution, Gevorg recognised that political independence was required, Abrahamian noted, and also that 'reform should begin from within not without'.[*] Extracts from

THE NEW
ARMENIA

Established as "ARMENIA" in Boston, Mass., under the Editorship of Arshag Mahdesian and the Honorary Editorship of Julia Ward Howe, Alice Stone Blackwell, Charlotte Perkins Gilman, Lucia Ames Mead, Rev. Charles Gordon Ames, Edward H. Clement, Prof. Albert S. Cook, Ph. D., L. H. D., Rev. Charles F. Dole, Rabbi Charles Fleischer, William Lloyd Garrison, Edwin D. Mead, Rollo Ogden, James Bronson Reynolds and Prof. William G. Ward.
European Honorary Editors: Anatole France, Georges Clemenceau and Victor Berard.

"Who can foretell our future? Spare me the attempt.
We are like a harvest reaped by bad husbandmen
Amidst encircling gloom and cloud."   "To serve Armenia is to serve civilization."
         JOHN CATHOLICOS   WILLIAM EWART GLADSTONE
    Armenian Historian of the Tenth Century.

| Volume XII. | SEPTEMBER, 1920 | No. 9 |

TABLE OF CONTENTS

his book were reproduced from September 1920 in four successive issues of *The New Armenia*, a Hunchak-supporting journal published in New York, bringing Abrahamian's name to a wider audience.

The book shows Abrahamian's perhaps studied vagueness about his exact ecclesiastical status. He was a higher vardapet (given in the book as 'supreme vardapet') but any claims he was a bishop or suffragan (assistant) bishop, or exercised episcopal functions remain unproven, even if other Armenian clergy did not contest his self-designation. The stick with a cross mounted with two serpents he was carrying in one of the photos in the book did indeed indicate episcopal rank in Orthodox Churches, but in the Armenian Church only the rank of vardapet or higher vardapet, representing their authority to preach and teach.

In 1920, Catholicos Gevorg – ever keen to expand the holdings of the library at Echmiadzin, despite the poverty in Armenia amid the post-Genocide refugee crisis – wrote to Abrahamian after hearing that the collections of the writer Raffi (whose widow Anna died in London that year) and the former priest of the Manchester church, Vardapet Sukias Baronian, might be available for purchase. Baronian, who had died in 1903, had worked on Armenian manuscripts, cataloguing

---

* *The Church and Faith of Armenia*, pp. 58-9.

those in the John Rylands Library in Manchester and the British Museum in London. Gevorg asked Abrahamian to find some rich benefactors who could sponsor the purchase of these collections 'and then to send them via a secure method to the Holy See'. He identified Boghos Nubar Pasha as a possible sponsor.[*]

For reasons that remain unclear, Abrahamian decided during his time in London to change his name to Nazarian (possibly the surname of his father, if Abel's son gave correct information at the time of Abel's death). The British secretary of state approved the change in December 1921. He gave his address as 6 Earl's Terrace, Kensington.[†] Presumably he had a room or flat in the elegant five-storey terraced house.

Armenian Politics

Court Circular.

BUCKINGHAM PALACE, March 9.
The Archbishop of Canterbury had an audience of The King this morning, and presented to His Majesty the Armenian Patriarch of Constantinople, who was accompanied by the Armenian Bishop of Manchester.

In early 1920 an Armenian delegation, led by Patriarch Zaven Der Yeghiayan, visited Europe, including London, to press the case for greater European protection for the Armenian population of the Ottoman Empire. Abrahamian was one of many guests (also including Nubar Pasha and Avetis Aharonian) attending a banquet for the Patriarch at the Carlton Hotel on 28 February.[‡] He translated for Patriarch Zaven in the meeting with King George V at Buckingham Palace on 8 March. 'The Archbishop of Canterbury had an audience of The King this morning,' the Court Circular noted the following day, 'and presented to His Majesty the Armenian Patriarch

---

[*] *Մայր աթոռ Ս. Էջմիածինը Առաջին Հանրապետութ յան տարիներին* (1918-1920 *թթ.*) (Mother See of Holy Echmiadzin during the First Republic (1918-1920)) (Yerevan, 1999), p. 450.

[†] *The London Gazette*, 3 January 1922, p. 48.

[‡] *Ararat*, 1920, pp. 10-11.

of Constantinople, who was accompanied by the Armenian Bishop of Manchester.'[*] Patriarch Zaven noted Abrahamian's presence at the meeting in his memoirs, but made no further comment on him.[†] Abel later recalled in *Why I Left* that King George had been 'sympathetic' to the Armenian people, but told the Patriarch that he has millions of Muslims in his empire, which influences Britain's dealings with the Ottoman Empire, remarks that Patriarch Zaven also recalled when he published his memoirs many years later.[‡] During the same London visit, Patriarch Zaven was also invited to dinner by the Bishop of London, Arthur Winnington-Ingram, and Abrahamian accompanied him.[**]

Also in 1920, Abrahamian hosted Bishop Khoren Mouradbekian, who passed through Europe on his way to the United States on a mission from Catholicos Gevorg V and the Armenian government. Khoren, who arrived in London in mid-March and stayed until 1 May, praised Abrahamian in a letter to Gevorg, declaring that he 'represents the Armenian clergy with honour in this important [Armenian] community, which is why the Armenians in general, and Boghos Nubar Pasha and Aharonian are so grateful to him'.[††] During this visit, Khoren and Abrahamian decided on the form of the Church's new Order of St Gregory the Illuminator. They organised the manufacture of the award in two categories, one for clergy and one for laypeople, with each having two classes. The pins were made of gold, silver, diamonds, rubies, emeralds and enamels in various combinations, depending on the classes, and about 100 are believed

---

* *The Times*, 10 March 1920, p. 19.
† Zaven Der Yeghiayan, *My Patriarchal Memoirs* (Mayreni Publishers, Barrington RI, 2002), p. 209.
‡ *Why I Left*, pp. 13-4. Der Yeghiayan, p. 209.
** Der Yeghiayan, p. 213.
†† Խորեն Ա. Մուրադբեկյան կաթողիկոս Ամենայն Հայոց (Հոգևոր գործունեությունը 1901-1938 թթ.) (Khoren I Mouradbekian, Catholicos of All Armenians (spiritual activity 1901-1938)), (Yerevan, 1996), pp. 81-6.

to have been produced. Some believe the awards were designed by the artist Arshag Fetvadjian, who was in London to organise the printing of Armenia's banknotes by London company Waterlow and Sons. It remains unclear which jeweller made the awards or who paid for the clearly expensive products. Abrahamian's three-yearly account of his activity, which he sent to the Catholicos on 5 August, made no mention of the production of the awards.

Order of St Gregory the Illuminator

Khoren arrived back in Britain in early August after achieving some degree of unity in the American Church, returning to Armenia in early October. In late October and early November, as the newly-named bishop of the United States, Tirayr Ter-Hovhannisian, was preparing to leave Armenia to take up his post, the chancellery at Echmiadzin prepared three envelopes to pass on for Abrahamian containing kondaks (encyclical letters). Abrahamian wrote to Khoren on 14 April 1921 to say he had received the three letters in early January when Tirair reached Paris. Abrahamian said he had personally read the fundraising kondak in London, Manchester and Marseille, Khoren told Catholicos Gevorg on 16 July, and also published it for wider distribution. Despite the 'terrible crisis', with many being 'on the verge of bankruptcy', Abrahamian expressed hope that 'the fundraiser will be successful, as Holy Echmiadzin has a great place in the hearts of the people and believes that in the near future it will have a considerable amount of money ready and will send it to Your Holiness in the safest possible way'. Abrahamian added that the awards were now ready, Khoren noted, 'but unfortunately Vardapet Abel is unable to send them. In accordance with Your Esteemed instruction, he handed one award with special ceremony to Captain [George] Gracey [of the British Military Mission], another award in accordance with Your Esteemed certificate was sent via Bishop Tirair to America'. Abrahamian had given an update on the plans to build a church in London with financing from Calouste Gulbenkian and had also reported that he had bought the library of the novelist Raffi for Echmiadzin, even though Boghos Nubar Pasha had declined to contribute to the cost.[*] On 1 August 1921, Catholicos Gevorg awarded the Order of St Gregory for laypeople, First class to Gulbenkian. The chancellery wrote to Abrahamian the following day instructing 'Your Honour from the awards in Your possession' to hand the relevant one to Gulbenkian together with the catholicos' kondak. Nazarian (as he was by now) finally handed over the award on 30 April 1922, as the construction of St Sarkis Church in London was already underway. Nazarian wrote to Echmiadzin that he had 'carried out the handover of the holy Catholicossal *kondak* and the appropriate award to the founder of St Sarkis Church of our city Mr Calouste Gulbenkian in his flat in the presence of a small circle of family members'. On 1 May, Nazarian sent off a package to Catholicos Gevorg with 100 of the various categories of the St Gregory the Illuminator award, as he wrote to Gevorg on 2 June. He said he still had a few of several, 'which I will send on at a convenient moment'. On 4 August – while visiting Constantinople – Nazarian again wrote to Gevorg expressing the hope he had received the latest documents 'and the remaining awards which a few days ago I sent from London'. It appears that nine of the awards Nazarian said he sent were missing from the package when it reached Echmiadzin.[†]

---

[*] ANA, f. 57, op. 3, d. 276, pp. 1-2.

[†] Amatun Virabyan, Nika Babayan, *Lists of Awardees 1918-1939* (Collage, Yerevan, 2011), pp. 119-21.

Abrahamian had numerous other church duties. He conducted the funeral of Anna Raffi, widow of the novelist, after her death in London in June 1920.[*] Following the death of Viscount Bryce in January 1922, Nazarian (as he now was) led a memorial service at the Savoy Chapel in central London.[†]

Ecumenism

Given his good education and wide knowledge of languages (in addition to Armenian he knew Russian, German, French and English and possibly others), Abrahamian was an obvious choice to represent the Armenian Church in the fledgling ecumenical movement. He had already become involved in the activity of the Anglican and Eastern Churches Association in London, attending a joint service at the city's St Paul's Cathedral on 18 December 1919 with the Anglican bishop of Northern and Central Europe and a prominent Serbian bishop. The London journal *Ararat* noted that 'among those who took part in the long and imposing procession of mitred prelates, cantors and clergy, one of the most striking figures was that of the Armenian Archimandrite, Dr. Abel Abrahamian'.[‡]

The Church of England was keen to expand ties with many other Christian Churches, particularly Orthodox and Oriental Churches. Exploratory proposals for intercommunion were put to representatives of these Churches in early 1920, and Abrahamian was the obvious local person to represent the Armenian Church's viewpoint. He met members of the Separated Churches Sub-Committee (which covered the Oriental Churches) of the Eastern Churches Committee in London on 26 April. After the meeting, the Sub-Committee – which had also consulted the bishop of Yerevan and unnamed others – reported that the Armenian Church was likely

---

[*] *The Times*, 21 June 1920, p. 18.
[†] *The Times*, 31 January 1922, p. 15.
[‡] *Ararat*, November/December 1919, pp. 588-9.

to accept mutual communion in emergency, though not with the Catholic or non-episcopal Churches. Church representatives had added that as soon as peace was established in Armenia, the Church intended to convoke a synod to resolve 'pressing problems' and reform church services. The Armenians admitted that they did not know the Anglican Church well.[*]

Abrahamian's ecumenical role soon extended internationally. He was chosen as the sole representative to attend a meeting of the World Conference on Faith and Order, held in Geneva in August 1920, together with leading Anglican, Lutheran, Orthodox and Free Church representatives. Abrahamian was billed as 'Armenian Bishop of London' and listed under the address of the Armenian Church in Upper Brook Street in Manchester. He was soon elected to the 17-strong organising committee of the conference and was also, together with Archbishop Yegishe Tourian 'of Constantinople', elected to represent the Church on the Continuation Committee which was to take the ecumenical initiative forward. Abrahamian's one recorded intervention at the Conference was to declare publicly that his Church wanted to associate itself with a resolution supporting Orthodox Church insistence that as moves towards greater unity moved forward, no attempts were to be made by one Church to poach members of others.[†] He expressed frustration in his 1924 booklet *Why I Left* about how the Armenian Church leadership was unable to give him direction over his participation in the Conference and its aftermath. In the wake of the Conference he wrote to both Echmiadzin and Constantinople, seeking answers on: 1. How to

[*] Lambeth Palace Library, MS 3909, pp. 40, 53-4.
[†] *Report of the Preliminary Meeting at Geneva, Switzerland, August 12-20, 1920* (World Conference on Faith and Order. Continuation Committee, 1920), pp. 2, 80, 82. Three letters between Abrahamian and Robert Gardiner, secretary of the Commission for the World Conference on Faith and Order, dated between 15 July 1920 and 14 May 1921, are in the World Council of Churches archive, Geneva, Box 23.0.003/1.

understand the concept of 'united church'?; 2. Is it essential to have a unified creed for the faith (common creed)?; 3. Is apostolic succession essential for the united church (i.e. ordination)? But months passed and 'I never received' an answer from either, he complained. One day while in Paris, he asked a priest from Constantinople why his letter remained unanswered. The priest responded that a member of the Religious Council had told him that 'we do not have a qualified person who could answer such questions'. A year later, Echmiadzin and Constantinople, having consulted each other, 'sent me a meaningless one-page text which I found inappropriate to present to the executive committee of the Conference – I did not wish to expose the intellectual poverty of our clergy to the world'.[*]

When news of the capitulation of independent Armenia's Dashnak-led government to Bolshevik forces in late 1920 quickly reached London, Abrahamian was seriously alarmed. In early December, within days of the takeover, he sent a telegram to the Archbishop of Canterbury, Randall Davidson, which was reported by Reuter's news agency. 'In my own name and that of the community,' he told the Archbishop,

> ARMENIAN APPEAL AGAINST SOVIET RULE.
>
> ——
>
> **" RUIN OF THE CHRISTIAN CHURCH IN THE EAST."**
>
> Reuter's Agency learns that the following telegram has been sent by Dr. Abel Abrahamian, the Armenian Suffragan Bishop of London, to the Archbishop of Canterbury:—
> "In my own name and that of my community I appeal to your Grace in our distress at the establishment of a Soviet regime in Armenia. Christianity in the East has been subjected for many centuries to the oppression of the Red Sultans, and now, when we have been rejoicing in the hope of its liberation from that yoke, with the assistance of our European Christian brethren, it has fallen into the power of the Red Army. We pray that the Christian world will not treat with indifference this event, which means the ruin of the Christian Church in the East."

> I appeal to your Grace in our distress at the establishment of a Soviet regime in Armenia. Christianity in the East has been subjected for many centuries to the oppression of the Red Sultans, and now, when we have been rejoicing in the hope of its liberation from that yoke, with the assistance of

---

[*] *Why I Left*, p. 11.

our European Christian brethren, it has fallen into the power of the Red Army. We pray that the Christian world will not treat with indifference this event, which means the ruin of the Christian Church in the East.[*]

Abrahamian built up close ties not only with the Archbishop of Canterbury but with other leading Anglicans in London. In July 1921 Abrahamian was able to ask the Archbishop to find out if the British Colonial Office would allow the embattled Catholicosate of Cilicia – seeking to leave the Turkish town of Sis as French forces were preparing to pull out – to relocate to Cyprus if that became necessary. Archbishop Davidson put the request to Lord Curzon at the Foreign Office, who assured him in August that the Colonial Office had heard from the government of Cyprus which 'could see no objection' to this. The following year, Catholicos Gevorg wrote to thank Archbishop Davidson for his sympathy 'towards the chronic sufferings, persecutions, and martyrdom of the innocent people of the land of Armenia and of our Church in the East'. Nazarian presented the letter and the award of the Order of St Gregory the Illuminator to the Archbishop in Lambeth Palace library in May 1922.[†] Archbishop Davidson remained highly concerned by the plight of Christians as the Ottoman Empire transformed itself into the Republic of Turkey. Archbishop Davidson asked his chaplain, Rev. George Bell (an enthusiastic ecumenist), to inform Rev. Henry Fynes Clinton, general secretary of the Anglican and Eastern Churches Association, that Nazarian was among those the Archbishop had consulted about the situation in Constantinople.[‡]

Nazarian's closest friend among the Anglicans was the priest John Douglas, a keen ecumenist who was particularly interested in and

---

[*] *Manchester Guardian*, 7 December 1920; *Pall Mall Gazette*, 7 December 1920.
[†] *The Times*, 26 May 1922, p. 18.
[‡] 21 October 1922 letter, Lambeth Palace Library, MS 3910, p. 70.

sympathetic towards the Eastern Churches, perhaps stemming from his short stint as chaplain to the British embassy in Constantinople in the early years of the twentieth century. For Christmas 1922, Douglas sent Nazarian a Christmas pudding. Nazarian wrote on 19 December 1922 to thank 'My dear Mr Douglas' for the gift 'which is really excellent'. And he added, with no trace of irony: 'I hope that one day you will receive from me in Armenia our Christmas keck [sic].' He took the opportunity to tell his friend of the consecration of St Sarkis, due on 11 January 1923, lamenting that time was too short 'for us to make a big ceremony of it, therefore we will do it very quietly'.

London Community

In a clear sign of his personal ambitions, Nazarian had pushed the Church's leaders to appoint a representative to the Church of England. In his 1922 book about the building of St Sarkis church, he stressed what he saw as the importance for the Armenian Church of Europe and above all London, 'the capital of the British empire and the seat of the head of the Church of England, the Archbishop of Canterbury'. Indeed, he described the city as 'the capital of Europe', requiring an Armenian church to be built. But he went far beyond that, viewing the Archbishop of Canterbury – 'the second personage after the king' – as a useful conduit to increase the Armenian Church's influence and which, therefore, necessitated the nomination of a permanent representative in London. In 1921 he had proposed just such a post in a letter to Patriarch Zaven of Constantinople who, he said, had been aware that it was thanks to the Archbishop of Canterbury that he had gained an audience with the king. 'We have today all the assurances from Lambeth Palace about the acceptance of such a representative.' He also regarded the Anglican Church as a model for reforms of the Armenian Church which he viewed as necessary. 'In truth, the observer's eye cannot fail to see that, at the cost of little effort, it is possible to borrow many things from this Church and adapt them to our situation and make them ours.' The representative of the Armenian Church 'who arrives in London' could form 'a bridge' between the two Churches.[*] Clearly Nazarian had himself in mind for the role.

Despite Nazarian's attempts to jump the gun by describing himself as bishop, in early 1922 Catholicos Gevorg charged him with forming a European diocese. Nazarian wrote to Armenian communities across Europe setting out his new mission.[†] But some were sceptical. Patriarch Zaven of Constantinople wrote to Gevorg on 17 February expressing doubts that Nazarian would be able to fulfil this task, stressing the unwillingness of individual communities to devote the funds needed for this and the differing loyalties of the communities.[‡]

Nazarian had dealings with (though appears not to have been close to) one of London's leading Armenians, the oil magnate and financier Calouste Gulbenkian. After Catholicos Gevorg V awarded the Order of St Gregory the Illuminator First Class to Gulbenkian on 1 August 1921, it was Nazarian who handed over the award to him on 30 April 1922.[**] When Calouste's son Nubar decided to get married in early 1922 – against his father's wishes and in a registry office – Calouste afterwards 'insisted on a religious ceremony according to the rites of the Armenian Church', as Nubar later recounted. Nazarian duly obliged. St Sarkis' Church had not been completed and the nearest churches were in Manchester and Paris. 'So the Armenian priest in London, the Reverend Nazarian, came to our first married home, a suite on the fourth floor of the Ritz Hotel. The service was held in the

---

[*] *St Sarkis*, pp. 16-8.

[†] Գեորգ Ե Սուրէնեանց կաթողիկոս ամենայն Հայոց (1847-1930 թթ.) (Gevorg V Sourenyants, Catholicos of All Armenians (1847-1930)), (Yerevan, 2005), pp. 538-9.

[‡] Ս. Ս. Սահակ Հասպայեան կաթողիկոս Կիլիկիոյ (1891-1940 թթ.) (His Holiness Sahag Khabaian, Catholicos of Cilicia (1891-1940)), Yerevan, 1997), pp. 362-4.

[**] Amatun Virabyan, Nika Babayan, *Lists of Awardees 1918-1939* (Collage, Yerevan, 2011), pp. 2-3.

Blessing St Sarkis' foundation stone, Nevarte
Gulbenkian on left (Pathé)

sitting-room. A table was brought in and a white tablecloth, usually used for breakfast, was laid on it. Candles were added and the table became an *ad hoc* altar.' Nazarian joined the couple and their two guests afterwards for champagne.[*]

Building St Sarkis

Nazarian's work to ensure the financing, building and completion of St Sarkis' Church in the Kensington district of London – the first, purpose-built Armenian church in the city and only the second in Britain (after Manchester) – was by far his most visible and enduring contribution to Armenian community life in the city. Indeed, Nazarian clearly set great store by it, as shown by the book he published about it in Paris in 1922 (before the consecration had even taken place). The book includes a diagram of the floor plan, a line drawing of the bell-tower at Haghpat Monastery in Armenia on which the design of the church was based, and correspondence in

---

[*] Nubar Gulbenkian, *Pantarœxia* (Hutchinson, London, 1965), p. 79.

English and Armenian about the building work, including with Calouste Gulbenkian.

The young priest appears to have been the initiator – or at least the most visible promoter – of the cause of building an Armenian church in London. At meetings in the capital he collected £6,650 in donations, which was enough to secure the freehold of the site where the church was eventually built, close to High Street Kensington in a fashionable area of London. However, fundraising stalled. Abrahamian then brought in Calouste Gulbenkian, travelling to Paris to outline his appeal in person. Gulbenkian welcomed the plan, but insisted that for him to fund it he would have to be the sole provider of the cost, which should not exceed £15,000 (including the cost of the land) and that the money already collected should be returned or transferred to a separate endowment fund, that the church should be named Surp Sarkis and be dedicated to the memory of his father, and that it be built 'on the lines of the Armenian Architecture about which I have spoken to you'. Following the meeting, and doubtless to ensure that his wishes were adhered to exactly, Gulbenkian put them in writing in a 10 January 1921 letter, written from his Quai d'Orsay home in Paris, to 'Very esteemed and dear Dr Abrahamian'. Gulbenkian concluded his letter by emphasising that 'had it not been for your personal and strenuous efforts in this direction, I would have deemed this work to be premature having regard to the sad state of our general national conditions'.[*] Gulbenkian and Nazarian – as he was by then – were among the original trustees of the church.

The two men chose the Haghpat monastery bell-tower as the basis for the design after examining the books *Die Baukunst der Armenier und Europa* by Josef Strzygowski, published in 1918, and *Armenia: Travels and Studies* by H. F. B. Lynch, published in 1901.[†] In November 1921 the London architectural firm of Mewes and Davis

---

[*] *St Sarkis*, pp. 26-9.
[†] *St Sarkis*, p. 39.

was engaged, and Arthur Davis prepared the design. After the design was completed speedily, a contract was signed with the building firm Holloway Brothers on 23 December 1921. A vicarage was also built next to the church.

On 11 February 1922, Nazarian blessed the foundation stone, which was laid by Nevarte Gulbenkian, wife of the benefactor. The cameras of Pathé were there to record the moment, presented in a short, silent film with the slightly inaccurate title 'First Armenian Church in England – Foundation stone laid by Armenian Supreme Vardapet with picturesque ceremonial'.[*]

During his initial years in London, Nazarian had led the community in worship in the chapel of the Sisters of the Church in Randolph Gardens in Kilburn in North London, and appears to have built up a good rapport with members of this Anglican order. In February 1922 – shortly after the blessing of the foundation stone for St Sarkis at which at least some of the sisters had been invited guests – the Mother Superior Adèle wrote Nazarian a warm letter. 'I am looking forward to the consecration in September,' she said. 'How glad you will all be to have your own church. We shall miss you here after all these years. We have been so glad for you to come, it seemed as if it were a little step toward the Reunion we are all longing for.'[†]

Nazarian continued to work closely with Calouste Gulbenkian as construction of the church proceeded throughout 1922. On 11 July 1922, Gulbenkian wrote to his agent in Constantinople, Dikran Tourabian, to inform him that Nazarian would be visiting the city to purchase items for St Sarkis.[‡] Nazarian was already in Constantinople by early August.

---

[*] https://www.britishpathe.com/asset/46195/.

[†] *St Sarkis*, pp. 59-60. Gulbenkian's letter is in Calouste Gulbenkian Foundation archives, Lisbon, LDN00450.

[‡] Calouste Gulbenkian Foundation archives, LDN00519. Correspondence between the two for 1921 is in LDN00404 and for 1922 in LDN00462.

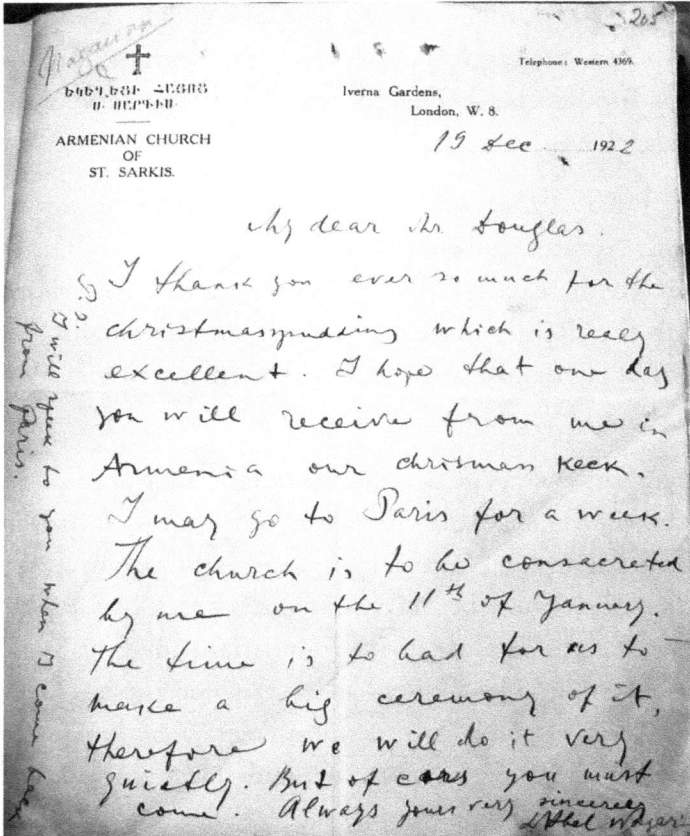

The consecration of St Sarkis on Thursday 11 January 1923 was a ceremonial affair. Ahead of the event, the secretary of the church's trustees prepared a programme for the event, sharing it with Rev. Douglas of the Church of England. The ceremony was due to begin at 10:30 am with the procession from the vicarage next door to the new church, singing the hymn 'All Holy Trinity' before entering by the west door (opposite the altar). Accompanied by the hymn 'Open the Door of thy Mercy', the women were to enter first and then the men. After the consecration and incensing of the altar, to the accompaniment of the hymn 'Thine Altar, O Lord', the interior pillars of the church were to be anointed before processing outside to anoint the lintels of the doorways on each side. The congregation then was to process from the west door right round the outside of the church before coming back in. Candles were then to be distributed to all. The curtain of the altar was to be closed as it is prepared, then when it is opened the candles are to be lit. A short sermon, the gospel and the creed follow, and then the liturgy. 'After the Mass at 1:15, those present are invited to a lunch at Kensington Palace Mansions by the wife of the benefactor, Mrs. Nouart Gulbenkian,' the draft programme ran. 'This programme must be accepted as an invitation.'[*]

On 10 January, the day before the ceremony, the Archbishop of Canterbury Randall Davidson wrote to Nazarian proclaiming 'my keen interest' in the consecration the following day.

> That this work should have been completed at a time when the sympathies of all thoughtful Christian people are awakened by the sorrows, the sufferings and the strain of the Armenian people is a matter of great thankfulness and we must all appreciate the generosity of the munificent donor. Pray be assured of my fellowship with you in this undertaking, my satisfaction that the Armenians in London should have such a centre of worship, and my earnest prayers that the Divine Blessing may rest upon the ministrations in the new church.

The same day, the Bishop of London Arthur Winnington-Ingram also wrote to Nazarian, addressing him as 'Brother', and noting that he was away from London. 'May I send you my blessing and my sincerest wishes and prayers that a happier time may dawn upon your oppressed race,' he told him. 'You are indeed martyrs for Christ's sake.'[†]

The consecration itself was recorded in detail by the Anglican paper the *Church Times*.

---

[*] Lambeth Palace Library, Douglas Papers, Vol. 61, pp. 206-8.
[†] *The Christian East*, May 1923, p. 85.

The ceremony of consecration, which was performed by the Vardapet-Episcop, Dr. Nazarian, consisted in the first place of bringing in the altar slab to be fixed upon the holy table, its unction with Chrism, blessed with the famous Holy Atch, *i.e.*, the relic of the right arm of St Gregory of Armenia, at Etchmiadzin by the Catholicos, and then of the anointing the consecration crosses upon the walls with the same Chrism. Music lovers and liturgiologists would have been deeply interested in the ancient distinctive Armenian melodies and the ritual of the ceremony. The Rev. G.K.A. Bell and the Rev. Harold Buxton, representing the Archbishop and the Bishop of London, read the Gospel, which was repeated at each of the many unctions, in English, and the Rev. J. A. Douglas in Armenian. The Liturgy followed.

During the liturgy the kondak from the Catholicos was read, as were the messages of greeting from the Archbishop of Canterbury and the Bishop of London. [*]

Another account appeared in *The Christian East*, a journal published in London by the Anglican and Eastern Churches Association, which noted that

> there was great dignity in the procession, in which the central figure was the Vardapet vested in a large mitre of Western form and glorious *schourdcharr*, surrounded by singers and acolytes in albs and maroon capes, served by the Priest Iltis as deacon, and accompanied by three English priests, the Rev. G. K. A. Bell, our Archbishop's Chaplain, the Rev. Harold Buxton, and the Rev. J. A. Douglas, in choir vesture. The whole made a fine picture.

The account, apparently by someone 'privileged to be at the consecration' of the 'little gem' of a church, also described the attendees.

---

[*] *Church Times*, 19 January 1923, p. 54.

St Sarkis, c. 1924

The souls of broken men need binding as much as their bodies need the Samaritan's care. And truly, as we chatted with men and women, lads and girls, among the 150 Armenians who crowded the stately little building, it was clear that Mr. Gulbenkian had spent his money more wisely than if he had given it (he has been very generous also in that matter) in material relief. Here was a fifteen-year-old village lad from Kharput with never a relation left alive. He had survived the death march to the Euphrates but had *seen* the way his mother and sisters died. There was another, eighteen years old, from Van, who had passed through the harrow himself. There was a woman from Smyrna. The priest who assisted Dr. Abel Nazarian in the consecration was from Moosh. Eight years back he was a husband with four sons. Now, he was alone. And so on. It is a martyr race, the Armenian! Verily it was good to see them meet, to hear them sing the songs of their Liturgy 'in a strange land' and to know that for a moment they were home. *

Pathé cameras returned to St Sarkis to record the consecration. Their short silent film shows the procession from the vicarage next door to the newly constructed church, with Nazarian accompanied by Rev. George Bell as well as robed acolytes, as a policeman stoically looks on amid what appears to be fog or smog. The film also shows Nazarian climbing a ladder to anoint the lintels of the doorways into the church. The title to the sequence, repeating the earlier inaccuracy, read 'First Armenian Church in England – consecrated with elaborate and picturesque ritual'. † The completed church was adorned with a plaque, which declared:

To the everlasting memory of his beloved parents, Mahtesi

---

* *The Christian East*, May 1923, pp. 83-5.
† https://www.britishpathe.com/asset/49885/ and https://www.britishpathe.com/asset/100713/.

Church consecration (Pathé)

Sarkis and Dirouhi Gulbenkian, this Holy Church of St
Sarkis was erected with devotion and love for his country
by Caloust Sarkis Gulbenkian, during the Patriarchate of
His Holiness George V Catholicos of all Armenians and
the pastorate in London of the Supreme Vardapet Abel
Nazarian LLD., in the Year of our Lord 1922 and of the
Armenian Era 1372.

Blessed be their memory!*

Scandal

Nazarian's career had up till now been rapid. From his remote village
on the fringes of the Russian Empire he had successfully graduated
from Echmiadzin seminary, undergone ordination, been raised to
become a vardapet, had after studies at Marburg completed a
doctorate at Zurich University and was widely respected and visible
as the head of the Armenian church in Britain. However, rumours
about Nazarian were beginning to swirl. As if in passing, in a 15
November 1921 letter to Catholicos Gevorg he expressed anger about
rumours that he was intending to resign from the priesthood. He
insisted to the Catholicos that these were 'completely groundless and
even intentional'. And, he implored him, 'please, Your Holiness, do
not pay attention to such rumours'.†

Yet scandal was soon to erupt. On the evening of Monday 5 February
1923, less than four weeks after St Sarkis' Church's consecration,
when he was 34 years old, Nazarian eloped to Paris with Satenig
Gulbenkian (born Satenig Ashkian in Alexandria, Egypt), wife of
church trustee Nerses Gulbenkian. The Gulbenkian couple – who
had been married by Roupen Kapikian in the Armenian church in
Alexandria in July 1912 – were the parents of a twin boy and girl born
in London in September 1913 (the girl, Virginie, had died soon after

* *St Sarkis*, p. 56.
† Quoted in *On the Occasion of...*, p. 13.

birth and the boy, Boghos, 14 years later, after Satenig had departed) and another daughter, Vergin, born in February 1916. Vergin had marked her seventh birthday just three days before Satenig and Abel's abrupt departure.

The scandal immediately hit the diaspora press. A London-based Armenian, who had just arrived in Paris from London, gave the newspaper *Artsakank Parizi* (Echo of Paris) a vivid account of the couple's departure on 5 February, which it published ten days later.

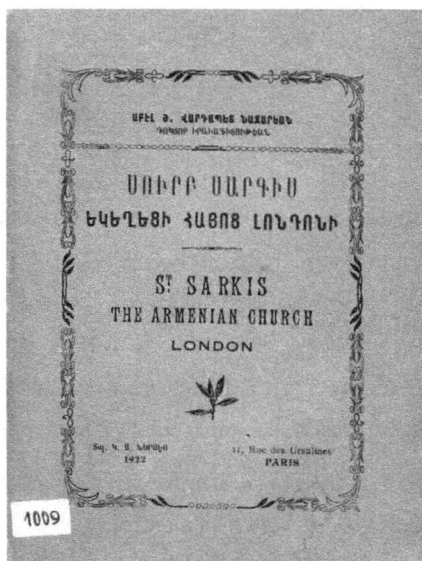

> On the evening of 5 February, a large covered [sic] automobile stops in front of the newly-built vicarage of the Armenian Church. An elaborately dressed young woman is sitting in the car. Abel vardapet, instead of his former semi clerical black garb and cylindrical hat is dressed in light grey *chic* style looking like a millionaire and his head covered with a soft *trilby hat*. *The only remaining feature from his former clerical status was his carefully-trimmed reddish beard, which indicated that the person was once a vardapet. He places all his belongings onto the automobile and then the clergy-layman, sitting side by side with a rich Armenian woman, speedily departs from the newly consecrated Armenian holy place.*
>
> *Abel vardapet and his lover escape London and come to Paris; but it is not known where they escaped to from Paris.*
>
> *Calouste Gulbenkian was extremely angry over this scandalous act and had the church closed.*

The miserable husband of the kidnapped woman, when he finds out that the woman he loved has escaped with the mischievous clergyman, starts to cry like a child, groaning 'what will happen to my poor children?' To give an idea about felonious Abel vardapet, let us note that the deceived husband was his [Abel's] long time principal defender and sponsor and had opened the doors of his home widely before him. This is how the Judas vardapet had rewarded his beneficent master.

The article – which speculated that the Catholicos would defrock Nazarian 'immediately' – was entitled 'An Armenian Woman Abducted by the London Pastor Senior Archimandrite Abel', with the subtitle 'St Sarkis Church Closed'. This is followed by a quotation from the 19th century Armenian satirist Hagop Baronian: 'Under the black cassock a pure heart cannot be found'.[*]

The New York newspaper *Hayastani Kochnak* (Bell of Armenia) reproduced the Paris article in its 24 March 1923 issue. It also added an editorial, which identified Nazarian by name but not Satenig or Nerses Gulbenkian.

> One of the leading Armenian merchants in London, a respected personality, a member of a grand family well-known for their philanthropy and patriotism, used to often welcome Abel vardapet to his house as a friend, pastor and teacher of Armenian to his two children. It is that friend, pastor and teacher who reveals his true character as a wolf in sheep's clothing; he seduces the lady of the house, an inexperienced young woman, and eventually snatches her from the hands of her husband and children. That Judas, with his deceived victim, travels to Paris, and ignoring the advice and grievance of the local pastor, Archimandrite Vramshapuh vardapet [Kibarian], continues to Berlin.

[*] *Artsakank Parizi*, 15 February 1923, p. 4. The paper frequently covered developments in later issues.

The editorial did plead for an end to the rule of celibacy for senior clergymen of the Armenian Church but, echoing a widely-held view, described Nazarian as a 'disgraceful vardapet'. 'This is the first incident in memory where an Armenian clergyman stoops to this level of mischievousness, by ignoring human conscience, moral laws, religious vows, national pride – and ultimately by trampling everything sacred.'[*]

Artsakank Parizi also took another look at Nazarian's book on St Sarkis, published in Paris the previous year (before the consecration had taken place).

> The success of constructing this building is the result of Abel vardapet's cleverness, therefore, driven by a desire to give a brilliant historical contour to his achievement, in the pages of his book he presents the London Armenian community in such unrealistic, exaggerated and grandiose terms that an outside Armenian reader would think that London is the Babylon of the Armenians, where one would see representatives of Armenians from every city and village where Armenians live in the Caucasus, Turkey, Egypt, Persia and India, with their characteristic features and varieties of dialects. Indeed, it is a simple fact that in this large city of about 9 million [sic] people, the number of Armenians is barely 100 to 150; it is difficult to imagine such a lost and unnoticeable Armenian community in any other place than in London.

The paper grudgingly admitted that Nazarian's drive had enabled the church to be built. 'Although this section of the book is peppered with self-praise, boasting and poetic whiff, had it not been for Abel vardapet, today there would not have been this beautiful example of Armenian Church architecture in London.' Yet 'London's clever

---

[*] *Hayastani Kochnak*, 24 March 1923, pp. 356-7. See also Joan George, *Merchants in Exile: the Armenians in Manchester, England, 1835-1935* (Taderon Press, Reading, 2002), p. 195.

pastor, just as he had shown a love for exaggeration, had likewise and regrettably shown signs of unchristian revenge in this book', the paper claimed, pointing to Nazarian's coverage of the ceremony of the laying of the foundation stone in February 1922.

> During that sacred ceremony, the previously designated eight individuals signed as witnesses of the foundation at the bottom of a specially prepared parchment, one of which was Mr. Nerses Gulbenkian. This name does not appear in the reproduced version of this document published in the book. Perhaps, that signature is erased even from the original official document.[*]

Indeed, the trust deed of settlement published at the end of the book (presumably before it had been signed, as it leaves blank the date to be signed in January 1923) lists only seven trustees, including Calouste Gulbenkian and Nazarian.

In the Soviet press, Nazarian was also the subject in 1923 of a withering sketch by Ler Kamsar (real name Aram Tovmaghyan), the Van-born satirist who had earlier studied at Echmiadzin seminary.

[*] *Artsakank Parizi*, 15 February 1923, p. 5.

Kamsar appears to have derived his material from reports in the diaspora press.

> At the end of 1919, Abel Vardapet Nazarian went to London as priest. He did not worry about housing, because the 'spiritual flock' of London would think about it. All he had to do to live happily was find a wife, and he took on the task of finding one himself. In order to achieve his goal, he brought to the fore the issue of building a church, drawing the people's attention away from their wives.

> And while Father Abel, on the one hand, would show Calouste Gulbenkian the path to heaven, by which, if he undertook to bear the expenses of the church, he would enter the kingdom, on the other, he would try to convince himself that the path leading to the real kingdom was the one leading to Gulbenkian, his wife. And so, in the early 1920s, in London, in two directions, there was a vigorous struggle.

> On the one hand, in one of London's 'convenient squares', hundreds of workers were digging the foundation of the Sarkis Church, on the other, Father Abel and Gulbenkian's wife were deepening their love in London's Kensington Park.

The sketch – accompanied by two cartoons of the besotted couple by the artist Garo Halabian – was published in Kamsar's short 1924 book *Invalid Dead: Antireligious Sketches.*[*]

Nazarian's scandalous departure left the parish of St Sarkis in chaos. Calouste Gulbenkian and his fellow trustees moved the same month to remove Nazarian as a trustee. They also determined that in future they would no longer consult the congregation.[†] Calouste Gulben-

---

[*] Ler Kamsar, Անվավեր մեռելներ: Հակակրոնական ֆելխտոններ (Invalid Dead: Antireligious Sketches), (Petrat, Yerevan 1924), pp. 28-30.
[†] CGF LDN497. Quoted in Jonathan Conlin, 'Philanthropy without borders: Calouste Gulbenkian's founding vision for the Gulbenkian Foundation', *Análise Social*, 2010, p. 286.

kian had Nazarian's name expunged from the plaque at the church and closed the church for several years.

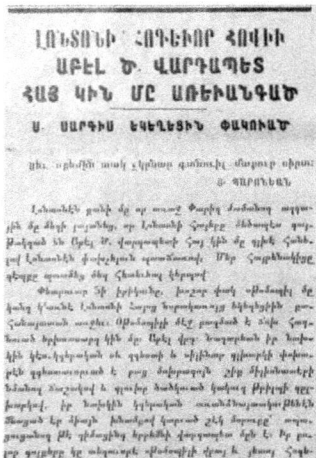

Artsakank Parizi (15 Feb. 1923)

The former Patriarch of Constantinople, Zaven Der Yeghiayan, who was looking for a new role in 1923, considered applying for the post of London pastor 'vacated because of the scandal surrounding Abel Vardapet' and sought the advice of Kapriel Noradungian. He wrote back on 6 April, promising to raise the prospect with Gulbenkian, but warned that 'from what I have heard, Mr. Gulbenkian is extremely annoyed by the well-known scandal and does not wish to hear any comments or remarks on matters having to do with the Church'. Noradungian also noted the after-effects of the scandal on the community, telling Zaven that 'we have heard that our co-nationals in London do not wish to frequent church as long as it has not been anointed by a worthy clergyman'.[*]

Nothing came of Zaven's idea to apply for the post and Nazarian was eventually replaced by Vardapet Krikor Goussan.

Meanwhile, Nazarian wrote to Catholicos Gevorg to explain his situation, posting his letter – which he said had been written on 5 February 1923, the day of his abrupt departure from St Sarkis – from the post office in Berlin. It reached the chancellery at Echmiadzin on 24 March, according to an annotation on the original letter.

---

[*] Der Yeghiayan, p. 259.

Your Holiness,

After a long spiritual struggle, today, with all seriousness, I come to inform Your Holiness that I am resigning from my priestly calling; I am resigning because I love someone and to whom I have decided to belong until death.

May the nation and Your Holiness be forgiving that I was able to serve only this much as an Armenian priest.

With the hope of serving the much-suffered Armenian people in my new life, I remain a humble [servant] of your Holiness,

ABEL NAZARIAN

(former Supreme Vardapet) member of the Brotherhood of Holy Echmiadzin[*]

Working for the Cheka

Echmiadzin defrocked Nazarian. He soon chose to work against the Church[†] and to return to Armenia, which he had not seen since long before the Soviet takeover, eventually boarding the train for Moscow in Berlin in early March 1924. Yet the year between his arrival in Berlin and his departure for the Soviet Union – as he was preparing and presumably negotiating his return with the Soviet authorities – remains shrouded in mystery. The Cheka, the Soviet secret police, appears to have devised the plan to use Nazarian against the Church from its censorship of all mail in and out of the country. The censorship body had passed on to the Cheka a letter Nazarian had written to a Hakob Haroutiunian in Yerevan, according to a 10 August 1923 report by Sergei Melik-Osipov, Petrosyan and Khachik Mugdusi on 'the activities of the church and the clergy and the means to use to combat them successfully'. (Haroutiunian may have been

[*] ANA, f. 57, op. 3, d. 523, p. 1. Reproduced in *On the Occasion of...*, pp. 14-5.
[†] For further background, see Felix Corley, *Catholicos and Commissar: The Armenian Church Under the Soviet Regime* (Gomidas Institute, London, 2025).

the Echmiadzin graduate who had also studied in Zurich at the same time.) The report quotes Nazarian's letter:

> I finally decided to leave the religious state and I recognise that religion, the faith and the clergy are leading us straight to destruction. After having lived for ten years in Europe, I have declared, and I am convinced, thanks to my own experience, that neither Europe nor the Armenians who live there (the same goes for those who live in Armenia) are favourable towards us. Although I have not yet been able to return to Armenia, I will soon come and propose my services to the workers of Armenia who have until now been deceived by the bourgeoisie and religion.

The Cheka concluded:

> This very characteristic letter aroused a certain emotion in the ranks of the black clergy [bishops and vardapets] and provoked anger against Abel, rendering him guilty of 'treason'. The harshest were mainly the bishops Karekin [Hovsepian], Bagrat [Vardazarian] and Mesrop [Ter-Movsisian] and the other vardapets, who are distinguished by their anti-revolutionary and reactionary convictions.[*]

In 22 February 1924, the presidium of Armenia's central committee proposed to the Armenian Cheka secret police, via the Soviet GPU secret police, to undertake measures 'to summon from abroad the former vardapet Abel Nazarian' to conduct subversive activity among the Armenian clergy. Once in the Soviet capital several weeks later, the GPU secret police began arranging for him to travel to Armenia 'for work on disrupting the clergy', in the words of Armenian central committee first secretary Aleksandr Shahsouvaryan. On 26 March 1924, Nazarian wrote from Moscow to Sahak Ter-Gabrielyan, Armenia's representative to the Transcaucasian republic. 'After a decade of service as a vardapet and as a representative of Echmiadzin,

---

[*] ANA, f. 1, op. 3, d. 230, pp. 32-5.

I have abandoned my orders and am now ready to stand side by side with our current government in the struggle with its internal and external enemies,' Nazarian declared. 'I am also convinced that my knowledge of facts of the activity of the Catholicos and his henchmen will give me the opportunity to help the work of the government to liberate the masses from religious ways of thinking.' The Armenian and the Transcaucasian Cheka were eager to get him working, with Melik-Osipov and Mugdusi asking Moscow on 18 April 'to speed up his arrival in Armenia to work on disrupting the Armenian clergy'.[*]

Returning to Yerevan soon thereafter (either with Satenig or to be joined by her separately), Nazarian threw himself into work against Echmiadzin. Fr Mesrop Melian, a leading clergyman in the church reform movement who openly collaborated with the Armenian Cheka, became the editor of the journal *Azat Yekeghetsi* (Free Church). The first issue of the 'religious-ethical and historical weekly' was published on 27 November 1924. Nazarian joined the editorial board that year. The journal, intended for priests and educated people, represented a rather mild form of anti-religious propaganda. Its print run did not exceed 1,000 copies and the periodical reached few readers. Articles were mostly taken from Russian newspapers translated into Armenian. For example, the first issue, which consisted of four pages, contained an article about the history of the Christian Church and a reprinted article from the first issue for 1924 of the *Christian* periodical from Moscow, in which the author attempted to seek causal relations between religion and science. The journal was published for only three years, with the final issue appearing in 1926.

Nazarian's apostasy was used more widely for the purposes of propaganda. The press published a profusion of articles about his departure from the Church, deeming his decision a manifestation of the attitude of an open-minded man who is aware of the 'inanity of

---

[*] Cheka documents from ANA, f. 1, op. 4, d. 10, p. 4; d. 24.

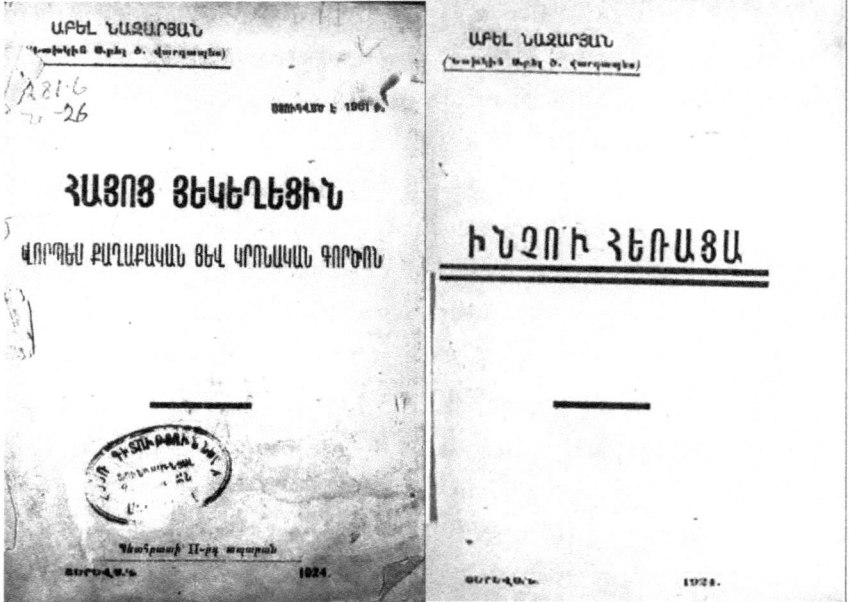

religion'. Abel himself published numerous articles in Soviet newspapers, including anti-religious ones. He often published under the pseudonym Marlen (presumably a contraction of the names Marx-Lenin).

Nazarian published an 18-page booklet in Yerevan in 1924 entitled *Why I Left*, where he set out his reasons for becoming a clergyman in the first place and his growing disillusion with the Church. He noted that 'many of us had blindly followed the Armenian church thinking that she is the true defender of the interests of our people and our ethnic civilisation'. He stressed that he was motivated to write his account as 'a moral duty that I am performing and not any personal reason'.

> I have nothing personal against the Armenian church, because not only has she not caused me any personal harm but, on the contrary, she had considered me an 'active' and 'worthy' clergyman, always speaking with honour and appreciation towards me. [...]

Indeed, life and years of experience, on the one hand, and the development of our scientific thinking on the other, have shown us that the Armenian church is not what we thought she is; therefore, disillusioned, many of us have left her at once. [...]

Today I would not have raised my pen to express my bitter experience to the public had it not been for the fact that this has implications for the public. [...]

I am fully convinced that none of us had decided to become a clergyman based on religious feelings; that is, we did not think of becoming a priest for the purpose of saving our and others' souls. As such, by saying that my disillusion has public implication, I wish to say that – having been in the leading ranks of the clergy for 12 years, having worked for her wholeheartedly, and by fighting against her opponents – I have finally come to the conclusion that the Armenian church not only has not served the interests of our society but, on the contrary, has been very damaging and will continue to be damaging as long as she exists.

The main attraction of becoming a priest for me, and for many others, was the Armenian church's public role.... [she] is called to offer vast and beneficial services to the nation.

Nazarian recalled his work in Europe after the end of the First World War and his 'interactions with the Armenian bourgeoisie' and high ranking clergy there.

I saw how the authority of the Armenian bourgeoisie and the Armenian clergy, hand in hand, are silencing and neutralising the clergyman [who is] protesting against the internal diseases of the church and her anti-people conduct. I saw how, in the final analysis, the Armenian church has turned into a powerful weapon in the hands of the Armenian bourgeoisie for the defence of its class interests. Finally, I saw how the Armenian church during the recent World War, having actively taken part in our national political issues, lewdly deceived our people for an entire decade without pity, by allying with the Armenian bourgeoisie and their loyal servants, the Armenian intellectuals of the former regime. [...]

.... she should have supported the party [i.e., Communists], under whose flag the Armenian working people are now living in peace and rebuilding their ruined homes. Even today, when it is beyond any doubt that the life and development of the Armenian people is possible only in the Soviet ranks and in the unity of socialist republics, the eyes of the Armenian church are abroad [Հայ եկեղեցու աչքը դուրսն է]; she still considers alien the regime in which the masses of workers in Armenia are breathing freely, who were barely liberated from yesterday's [recent] violence and exploitations. [...]

In view of all these, is it not possible to say that the Armenian church is a hypocritical institution?... Isn't it hypocritical that that institution is tolerating everything behind the curtain which is considered major profanity outside the curtain? Isn't it hypocritical for that institution, which preaches religion and faith through the mouth of her functionaries, who themselves are unbelievers? Isn't it hypocritical for that institution, which even as being the obedient and loyal servant of the bourgeoisie, presents herself as the defender of the downtrodden and the persecuted? Isn't it hypocritical for the clergy, who follow the principle of *'ub: beno ibi patria'* [sic] [*ubi bene ibi patria*] ("where it's good that is my fatherland") to present themselves as great patriots? Isn't it hypocritical for the clergy, who in reality, despite being more money-lovers than even money lenders, appear as selfless in the outside? [...]

It is not possible not to leave the Armenian church after seeing all these and being convinced on numerous occasions, when especially the church authorities and the bourgeoisie are readily vigilant to suffocate all protest and criticism which may be raised by the ranks of the clergy. [...]

The day is not far when the eyes of the Armenian workers will open and under the blows of their just anger, the Armenian church and the clergy will crumble once and for all, just as the Armenian capitalist and the bourgeois were crumbled.

It is at that time that the politically liberated Armenian workers will be liberated spiritually as well.

Nazarian recounted how he had responded to the kondak he had received from the Catholicos in 1921 to raise funds in Europe for Echmiadzin. As a result, he raised 1,500 British pounds and transferred it to the Catholicos through a friend in Britain who was due to travel to Armenia (although Nazarian does not identify him he was Anglican clergyman Hubert Harcourt, the director of the British orphanage in Yerevan).

When the British man who took the money to the Catholicos saw the horrible situation of the people [refugees who had fled the genocide] at the walls of Echmiadzin, the man suggested that part of the money be used to help these destitute people. But the Catholicos refused and wanted to have the entire amount for Echmiadzin. This is how worried the Armenian church is towards her naked and hungry flock.

Clearly, Nazarian was constrained in what he was allowed to say in a booklet published by a state-run press under a regime which imposed strong state censorship. *Why I Left* was eloquent and direct, but confused. He recounts how the Church treated him with respect, but in the same breath describes his experience as bitter. Nor does he explain why he now apparently felt that the Church caused harm to the nation. His booklet was much used in anti-religious propaganda.

Nazarian also published in Yerevan in 1924 another 16-page booklet, *The Armenian Church as a political and religious factor*, which went further than his other works in making the Church appear incompatible with Soviet life – and indeed a danger to it. It even argued that the Church in its current form should be destroyed.

'In the past,' Nazarian declared, 'many laymen and clergymen had revolted against the backward and shabby state of the Armenian church and made revelations about the mischievousness, thefts and inabilities of her clergy.' He went on to praise what he considered the much-improved conditions under Soviet rule, which he argued gave individuals the possibility to make their own choice.

> The freedom of religion declared by the Soviet authorities gives the right for the activity and free expression of opinion for or against religion and the church. In due course, the leaders of the Supreme Council of Echmiadzin had received permission to have even their own publication. Indeed, even those who advocate for reforms in the church or those who are in favour of complete liquidation of the church have freedom to express their views. The Armenian people, whether believers or non-believers, are placed in best conditions today because they are able to examine the essence of their church without outside prohibitions and are able to determine a position towards the church based on that examination.

Nazarian insisted that 'There is nothing in the Gospel that Christ preached which enables us to conclude that Christ dealt with politics', adding that 'on the contrary there is clear evidence that he distanced himself from political issues and instructed his followers [to do] the same'. He then moved to an attack on the Church leadership. 'The Armenian church has conveniently forgotten her purely religious status and from her beginning until today has dealt with political issues.'

> The Armenian church, in order to make her [political] behaviour pleasing and acceptable to the people, came up with the notion that she would take in her hands the political fortune of the Armenian nation and, through the intermediary of European Christian churches and states, recover the Armenian nation's lost political independence.

Nazarian claimed that throughout history, the Church 'changed her purely religious nature and willingly turned into a kind of political organisation'. He added: 'When a public institution abandons its true vocation and engages with issues that are not relevant [to that vocation], it cannot produce useful results, neither for the people nor to itself as an institution. Everyone has many wounds in his heart and soul caused directly or indirectly by the Armenian church, which are still not healed.' He then moved to attack the Church's insistence on clerical celibacy for all except parish clergy, perhaps motivated by his own relationship with Satenig.

> All rights and permission are concentrated in the hands of the celibate priesthood (catholicos, bishop, vardapet), while the secular clergy (married priests) have been left in the lowest ranks, deprived of all opportunities for reaching higher positions. This discrimination against the [married] priesthood is neither Christian nor Armenian.

Nazarian then makes a sweeping claim, with no supporting evidence: 'No other church's clergy have been as miserable as the Armenian church's.'

Blaming the alleged politicisation of the Church and internal 'discrimination', Nazarian complains that it 'has ceased to be a church and has turned into a mere place for rituals', while the people 'have turned into a mere ritualistic community, whose faith is exhausted completely by ritual worship'. He laments the demise of the sermon, 'the only instructing force of the religious-moral message'.

Nazarian is keen to stress how out of touch he feels the Church is with the new Soviet society. 'Although she is speaking in the name of the Armenian people, in reality she is defending the interest of the bourgeoisie.' He goes so far as to maintain that 'the Armenian church as an institution of leadership does not have a place in our current reality; indeed, its existence is at once superfluous and even dangerous.'

> It is clear that an institution that seeks the mediation of foreigners, like the Armenian Church, does not correspond to our current [Soviet] regime and pursues altogether different interests and serves different political aims.

> With these considerations, I would even venture to say that given her political perceptions, the Armenian church does not conform to our current regime, therefore, she is condemned to death.

After urging that the Church 'go to where the Armenian bourgeoisie rules', Nazarian stirred up concerns about how much the diaspora flock was influencing Echmiadzin.

> How is it possible that the head of the Armenian church sitting in Echmiadzin would not be influenced by the political views and intentions of his oversees 'flock', who are at once against the regime in our country and the ruling ideology? Whether she likes it or not, she has to consider the political attitude of the overseas Armenian bourgeoisie towards Soviet Armenia, especially as her own attitude is the same.

Nazarian regarded this alleged diaspora influence as one example of what made the Church's leaders 'dangerous to the interests of our country'.

He then moved on to argue for the destruction of the current Church and creation of a replacement, while holding back from attacking Christianity per se.

There is nothing left for the Armenian faithful who follows the religion of Christ but to sever his ties with the Armenian church and to create a religious organisation which would be in conformity to the current regime in our country and the spiritual needs of our people.

To preserve the Armenian church the way she is would mean causing the dead corpse to stink and burying later.

The Armenian church of today is rotten in her roots; she has poisoned the fount of the Christian religion, therefore, it is necessary to destroy the foundations of her dilapidated building so that we could reach the real source.

Arguing for a new evaluation of Christ's mission, Nazarian insisted that 'The believing Christian should establish a church that would improve his life; [a church that] would respond to his needs in life and serve him... Religion as such is not being destroyed, but its [physical] expression, the organisational form and is being changed because the church is not religion itself, but one of the possible expressions of it.' He then set out his vision of how the new Church should look.

To enable the new church to serve life, there should be a church community in it which is connected to life and not some kind of a hierarchy (clerical rank) which is cut off from life. And life is work. Whoever does not work, cannot enter a church community. Whoever does not live by his work, he cannot be a member of the new church. And because the [Church] hierarchy is living not by its but by others' work, as such she cannot have a place in Christ's church. The church cannot be a place of exploitation or source of subsistence for this or that class or an individual.

The principle of serving life implies that the living word of the Gospel and the worship of work will have central places in the new church, which shall replace the mindless and purposeless rituals of the Armenian church. And for the sermons and the worship of work to serve their purposes, they should be in a language comprehensible to the people, that is, in modern Armenian.

The new church should not have mystical sacraments nor the intercession of saints and worship, but she must simply establish a direct relationship between the believer and supreme religious-moral principles, to be guided along the path that Christ has drawn.

Echmiadzin hit back in 1925, publishing a response in Paris refuting Nazarian's claims about the Church and accusing him of moral failings. Interestingly, the 16-page booklet *On the occasion of former Vardapet Abel Nazarian's 'Why I Left' booklet. A publication of the Brotherhood of the Mother See of Holy Echmiadzin* was published by *Artsakank Parizi*, the Paris newspaper that had been so critical of Nazarian when he eloped in 1923. Presumably censorship prevented the booklet from being published in Armenia. 'Based on his written information, we would assume that after eloping with that woman and especially after coming to Soviet Armenia, perhaps he "finally was convinced" that the Armenian church is harmful, and therefore started to fight against the Armenian church, of course, again, "with his whole heart"...', the booklet notes sarcastically. 'One wonders what has compelled him to publish accusations, with a populist logic and full of falsehoods?' it adds. Echmiadzin's response quotes from his 1920 book *The Church and Faith of Armenia*, contrasting the quotes with his views as expressed just four years later in *Why I Left*. The response aims to give readers its own view of why Nazarian left the Church.

There is no room for doubt: he is resigning from his religious calling because he loves someone with whom he has decided to belong until death.

He had given a similar promise and vow of loyalty during his ordination to the priesthood. From his resignation letter it seems that he had felt a bit awkward, or perhaps shame, and therefore asking for the nation's and His Holiness's forgiveness.

This is why and how Abel Nazarian left.

How Nazarian's anti-Church articles were received in Soviet Armenia remains unclear. However, a late 1924 Armenian Cheka report mentions him as one of the most read and influential 'clergymen' in the region of Lori, whose activity would contribute considerably to an internal rift in the Armenian Church.[*]

Inside the Soviet Union, Nazarian's writings lived on long after his departure, helping to fill the pages of anti-religious publications. While such works were not intended as attacks on the faith, and were designed to criticise aspects of the way the Church functioned, their usefulness encouraged the state to promote them. Indeed, publications by Nazarian (and by fellow Free Church advocate Benik Yegiazarian) appear to be among the few works by Armenian authors recommended to readers of the new atheist magazine *Anastvats* (Godless), even as late as 1928 when the Free Church movement was close to being wound up. From 1928 to 1931 articles signed with Nazarian's name or, in the case of his articles in *Anastvats*, with his journalistic pen-name Marlen were regularly published.[†]

Back in Europe

In distant London, which Nazarian had abandoned in February 1923, Nerses Gulbenkian began proceedings to divorce his unfaithful wife Satenig. In February 1925, he presented his petition to the High Court in the Strand in London, alleging that his wife 'has frequently conducted adultery with Abel Nazarian'. In particular, he alleged that 'on or about the 1st day of January 1923 and on other dates between

---

[*] ANA, f. 1, op. 4, d. 24, p. 132, a hand-written note of the Cheka of Armenia 'According to an intercepted letter of 9 November 1924 …'.
[†] Marlen, 'Ejmiatsin and Dashnaktsutiun', *Anastvats*, No. 3, 1928, p. 1 and *Anastvats*, No. 9-10, 1931, pp. 9-12.

that date and the 5th day of February 1923 the respondent [Satenig] did at the Armenian Vicarage, Iverna Gardens, London W. commit adultery with the said Abel Nazarian and they are at present co-habiting and habitually committing adultery together at Erivan in the Republic of Armenia'. Nerses Gulbenkian maintained that his wife, 'domiciled in England', was at that point living in Yerevan, though he had no address for them. The petition was sent to both Satenig and Nazarian – instructing them to respond within 100 days – simply listing their address as Yerevan. A hand-written addition on the back of the petition from the solicitors in August 1925 notes that 'since the presentation of this Petition it has come to our Knowledge that the full address of the Respondent and Co-Respondent is: 4 rue Nazaroff, Erivan, Armenia'. This information seems to have arrived within a month of the original petition being filed, as on 25 March 1925 the notices were ordered sent to Satenig and Nazarian by registered post. A notice was also placed in *The Times*.[*] At the hearing on 7 December 1925 – which heard from Nerses Gulbenkian, a witness speaking in his favour and the evidence on affidavit of another witness – the judge issued a decree nisi, with custody of the two children going to Nerses Gulbenkian and the costs of the hearing to be borne by the co-respondent (Nazarian). The final divorce decree was issued on 14 June 1926.[†] The marriage entered into 12 years earlier in far-off Alexandria was over.

Whether or not Nazarian knew or cared about the divorce proceedings in London's High Court remains unknown. He and Satenig, according to his own account, married in Yerevan and it is in Armenia that she became pregnant. By the time the divorce was finalised they were long back in France, with one child already born

---

[*] *The Times*, 11 April 1925, p. 3.
[†] Nerses and Satenig Gulbenkian divorce papers from the High Court in London, 1925-6, are in The National Archives, London, J77/2162/7720.

and the second about to be born. Their daughter Soussane was born in Dijon on 11 September 1925.[*] Their son, Serob (who went by the French version of his name Serge), was born in Montfermeil near Paris on 2 April 1927. Interestingly, both children were named after Abel's parents.

Within months of returning to France in 1925, Nazarian had revived contact with Canon John Douglas, who took a close interest in the Eastern Churches and was in regular contact with Lambeth Palace. Nazarian's initial renewed communications with his old friend appear a little wary, perhaps as he was not sure how sympathetic Canon Douglas would still be towards him. However, a warm

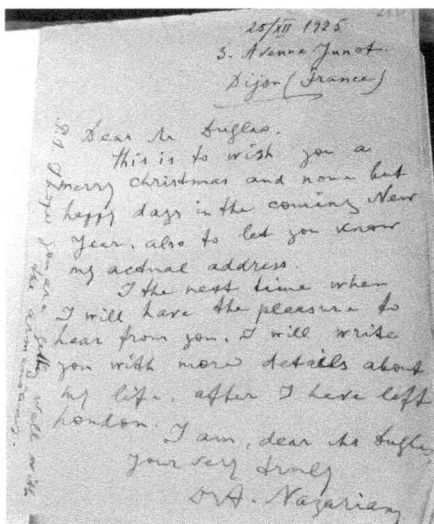

correspondence soon developed, in which Nazarian tried to present his activity in Soviet Armenia in the most positive light he could. Nazarian's first letter to Douglas was in English.

25 December 1925

3 Avenue Junot

Dijon

Dear Mr Douglas,

This is to wish you a happy Christmas and none but happy days in the coming New Year. Also to let you know my actual [current] address.

---

[*] Information from 10-year compilation of Dijon births, 1923-32, where her name is incorrectly spelled 'Nozarian'.

The next time when I will have the pleasure to hear from you, I will write now with more details about my life after I have left London.

I am, dear Mr Douglas, your very truly

A. Nazarian

P.S. I hope you are getting [on] well with the Armenians.[*]

Douglas responded on 1 January 1926, saying how 'delighted' he was to receive Nazarian's letter. While noting that he was in contact with the new vardapet who had replaced Nazarian, Krikor Goussan, Douglas insisted that 'no one takes your place to me'. And he added that 'having worked so long together, I value your friendship very much'.[†] Nazarian responded to Douglas in French.

13 January 1926

3 Avenue Junot

Dijon

My dear friend,

Your letter of 1st of this month gave me great pleasure. I was not able to reply earlier because of my absence and I ask you not to blame me.

I'm writing this letter in French as I know you like this language: but you may write to me in English.

How can I give you now in a letter the details of my life over the last few years? The details would be enough to fill several volumes. But I will content myself this time with recounting to you some of the principal episodes of this life which has been so interesting as much from a personal point of view as from a national and humanitarian point of view.

After renouncing my church rank in 1923 I decided to

---

* Lambeth Palace Library, Douglas Papers, Vol. 61, p. 210.
† Douglas Papers, Vol. 61, p. 212.

return to Armenia to be useful to my nation. As I was not ignorant of the difficulties I could have on the part of the current regime, the love of the homeland and the desire for public activity obliged me to demand permission for entering Russia. This permission was granted me and I boarded the train in Berlin for Moscow at the beginning of March 1924. Three days later I already found myself in the red capital. It was impossible to find lodging there which was more or less bearable. From there I took the train to Petrograd (pardon! Leningrad!) where I was able to hide myself in a hotel which had managed to preserve its bourgeois allure even though it was managed by the Petrograd soviet.

In these two main cities I got to know some ruling persons at the same time as I discovered the moral and material misery, stupidity and hypocrisy of the Soviet regime. After several months' study in Russia I left for Armenia. The government gave me a good welcome and they entrusted me with a good post. The misery that I encountered in Armenia largely exceeded that of Russia. Misery everywhere, among the peasants, workers, and in all classes of the population. This material misery was also associated with moral misery. The Armenian Church exists in name only. The new generation is completely degenerated in the new schools, where they teach only socialist doctrines and the movement of the working class in different countries. You can well imagine the rest. Freedom of speech and of conscience have been entirely destroyed and everyone is obliged to praise the new orders and the Soviet regime. This state of affairs, the general misery and my impotence as a non-communist obliged me to leave the territory of the Soviets. After demanding this for several months I was able to get permission to leave in May 1925 and this was thanks to the high-level protection on the part of one of my former pupils who is today a communist and government member.

So I left Yerevan to travel to Persia via Baku – Anzali [in Persia]. There I made contact with some Persian merchants as I was without money. Business obliged me to go to Tehran where after several months "business" I succeeded in saving enough money to return to France and to buy a property. The road from Tehran to Marseille was the most painful journey but the most interesting. From Tehran to Baghdad by car, from Baghdad to Beirut also by car through the desert. It was during this journey that I got to know the true Orient.

Here are some major lines of the life I have passed after leaving London. The greatest event of this life is that I married in Yerevan and I am already the father of a charming little girl. My family will soon be installed in the property I have most recently bought near Paris. Once installed I will let you know and hope you will come to see us.

Goodbye dear friend. Awaiting your news.

I am always your devoted

A. Nazarian[*]

Nazarian wrote again to Canon Douglas in May 1926 (this time in English) once he had moved to his new house in the Paris area.

29 May 1926

10 Avenue des Bégonias

Montfermeil

I am really ashamed that I have left you without news all this time. But of course this was not my fault. I was busy with my new house, which is now quite ready to receive

---

[*] Douglas Papers, Vol. 61, pp. 213-6.

such good friends like you. I have had it repaired and furnished not as one does in Soviet Russia but quite à la european [sic]. My garden is not as good as the Biblical Edem, but I am sure that a faithful servant of the Bible will like it too. I hope you will find time to come one day to the Continent – Paris, when you will see my charming wife and sweetest daughter in my new home. I am afraid that you will then decide to get married. It is never too late to do good things!

Au revoir mon cher ami and let me have of your good news soon.

Yours very affectionately

Dr A. Nazarian

All my compliments and good wishes for your new degree [in 1924 Douglas had become honorary canon of Southwark Cathedral]! I hope to call you one day my dear Bishop![*]

Despite his evident pride in his Montfermeil home, Nazarian soon put it up for rent or sale, with repeated small advertisements in the newspaper *Le Journal*. One in August 1926 described it as a beautiful property, 15 kilometres from Paris, close to the train and tram, with seven rooms plus bathroom, available both furnished and unfurnished. He placed a further advertisement in November 1926 at a much lower price, with a much smaller advertisement the following June.[†]

Second Thoughts?

Back in France, Nazarian appeared to be having second thoughts about his behaviour towards the Church. In 1927, he wrote from Paris

[*] Douglas Papers, Vol. 61, p. 217.
[†] *Le Journal*, 31 August 1926; 20 November 1926; 8 June 1927.

a letter of apology to Catholicos Gevorg for what he had said in his anti-Church publications.

10 Avenue des Bégonias

Montfermeil (S.O.)

France

10 February 1927

Your Holiness,

A belated announcement, which I make to Your Holiness. As it is said, better late than never.

I know that I have caused Your Holiness pain on two occasions. First, by resigning from [my] religious calling [priesthood] and then by publishing anti-church booklets and articles in Yerevan in 1924-25. It is not the first [reason] that is prompting me to write to Your Holiness, because my conscience is clear about that – 'whoever can carry, carries'. I carried as much as I could and then did not wish to fake it anymore, because 'No one can serve two masters'. And today we are happy, both my wife and I; our first born child was recently baptised in the Armenian Church in Paris. [However] it is not so [the case] with the second point I mentioned [above], about which today I am writing these lines driven by the moral obligation to explain. And that explanation, which is dictated by my conscience, I consider a duty to address it to Your Holiness as a Supreme Spiritual Father.

After I left the priesthood, the desire to serve my nation continued to remain vibrant in me. Based on the information I had been able to gather from outside, I decided to come to Armenia, being sure that I will be able to put my strengths in the service of improving the situation of my much-tortured nation. But, when I crossed within the Soviet borders, I realised that I had been deceived, as I found the reality to be completely different than what I had assumed. Indeed, it was under the pressure of that reality that I, like so many others, was exploited by those circumstances and people, who are ruling our country today, putting out a series of publications against my conscience and convictions. And today, as I am free from all kinds of obligations and brutalities, I inform Your Holiness that I am revoking and declaring void all the anti-church booklets and articles published under my name in Yerevan in 1924-25.

The [true] opinions and feelings I have towards the Armenian Church, the Mother See and the institutions under her auspices are not in the noted publications, but have found their genuine expressions in my works published abroad in German, English and Armenian, copies of which are found in the Library of the Holy See and I am the convinced defender of their content today and always.

Wherever and whatever I may be, the Armenian Church with her Mother See and her majestic incumbent [Catholicos] remain very close to my heart; likewise, as with many others like me, the memories of [our] *alma mater* the seminary, the sense of feeling so close to these [institutions] gives me the courage today to request from Your Holiness not to reject my wife's wish, by giving permission for our church wedding. As such, we will also be able to courageously fulfil the religious education of our children in the bosom of the Armenian Apostolic Holy Church.

Remaining the most humble servant of Your Holiness,

Abel Nazarian[*]

---

[*] ANA, f. 409, op. 1, d. 5371, p. 1.

Another letter full of accusations against Nerses Gulbenkian was sent to the Catholicos in Satenig's name on the same day, though the Eastern Armenian phrasing of many parts of it may indicate that Abel too had his hand in its composition.

> Two years ago, in dissolving my earlier marriage, the Supreme Spiritual Council of Echmiadzin deprived me of my right to undertake a religious marriage. This decision was taken without having listened to more details from me and based on a document written by my adversary which is, from start to finish, full of lies and accusations. The simple fact that I fled from this cursed family undermines by itself the content of this letter.

Satenig goes on to describe Nerses as repulsive and avaricious, complaining that he had 'poisoned her life'.

> My past and my current life, in which I am happy both as a wife and a mother of a child, testify to my moral integrity. Isn't the Church interested in seeing its flock composed of families founded on reciprocal love, respect and attention, rather than rotten and unstable marriages which either collapse under the slightest wind or, even if they endure, bring matrimonial happiness neither to one nor the other of the two parties, in addition rendering their children unhappy? Also, your Holiness, without going into the details of the question, I address your Holiness today to demand most humbly, even if I was obliged to sin against the laws of my Church, to allow me through your fatherly pardon to marry again through a new religious marriage to Abel Nazarian who I married in a civil ceremony some time ago.*

Although Echmiadzin received Satenig's letter, it sent no reply. So she wrote the same letter again on 26 August, noting wrongly that it 'had

---

* ANA, f. 409, op. 1, d. 5371, p. 2.

not reached its destination', though this time describing herself as 'a wife and a mother of two children' (Serob had been born in April).[*]

With no response to these letters, Nazarian approached Bishop Vramshapuh Kibarian in Paris to pass on a further appeal to Echmiadzin. Nazarian again complained in a 15 January 1928 letter about this lack of response to his earlier appeals sent by registered post. He begged for confirmation of receipt of the letters and a response to his appeal, whether positive or negative.[†]

However, Abel and Satenig's demands for the annulment of her marriage to Nerses Gulbenkian had taken on a wider significance, causing a breach between Echmiadzin and the Cilician Catholicosate as the two were trying to follow a policy of rapprochement.[‡] Catholicos Sahag was close to the Gulbenkian family, and the Cilician See had benefited from donations from both Calouste and Nerses Gulbenkian. Sahag repeatedly asked Gevorg and – after his May 1930 death – locum tenens Archbishop Khoren Mouradbekian not to grant Abel and Satenig's request. Yet behind the scenes Khoren (who Abel had hosted in London in 1920) and another bishop Bagrat Vardazarian seem to have been ready to release Satenig to have another religious wedding. On 4 September 1928, possibly without informing Gevorg, they prepared a short draft of a certificate on a piece of plain paper reading: 'This certificate is issued to Mrs Satenig Nazarian, resident in Paris, by His Holiness the Catholicos by which she is accorded the right of remarriage.' The draft notes that a certificate needs to be signed by the members of the Supreme Spiritual Council and the seal needs to be attached.[**] It remains unclear if this was merely a draft which Gevorg or the Supreme

---

[*] ANA, f. 409, op. 1, d. 5371, p. 5.

[†] ANA, f. 409, op. 1, d. 5371, p. 6.

[‡] Catholicos Sahag letter to Catholicos Gevorg, ANA, f. 409, op. 1, d. 4469, p. 13.

[**] ANA, f. 409, op. 1, d. 1371, p. 7.

Spiritual Council rejected, or if such a certificate was ever formally issued and sent.

In early 1930, on a visit to Paris, Nerses Gulbenkian got wind by chance of Echmiadzin's apparent readiness to consider allowing his former wife a second religious marriage. On 15 January he sent Catholicos Gevorg a virulent, eight-page letter, complaining that Nazarian had 'destroyed my harmonious family nest and turned my two young children into orphans' and attributing the death of his son Boghos to Satenig's abandonment of the family. Gulbenkian expressed his anger on learning that Abel had been 'secretly married religiously in accordance with the canons of the Armenian Church by Bishop Kibarian'. And he added: 'I consider this last act, that is the marriage of Abel Nazarian to the woman he abducted to be a greater sin than the abduction of my wife.'* Gaining no response, Gulbenkian sent a further telegram on 12 May asking for a response to his January letter, apparently unaware that Gevorg had died four days earlier.

Possibly at Satenig's behest, their daughter Soussane had been baptised by a priest of St John the Baptist Armenian church in Paris, Fr Parthog Takmejian, at their Montfermeil home on 7 July 1926. In a sign of Nazarian's continuing skill at attracting support from prominent individuals, the girl's godfather was Avetis Aharonian, a leading politician who had chaired the Armenian National Council in 1917-18 and had been speaker of the Armenian parliament from 1919-20 (and had met Abel in London in November 1919 and again in February 1920). The register of baptisms records the parents as Abel Nazarian and Satenig Ashkian and notes Soussane's 'illegitimate birth'. The register of baptisms was even more blunt over the baptism of Serob by Fr Takmejian in Montfermeil on 7 August 1927, four months after his birth. Nazarian is described as 'resigned Vardapet and priest of London', while Satenig is described as 'legal wife of Mr

---

* ANA, f. 409, op. 1, d. 4944, pp. 1-8.

Nerses Gulbenkian of London' (though under English law the two had by now been divorced). The baptism register notes: 'Out of wedlock illegitimate birth, should not be given a certificate.' Despite Abel and Satenig's repeated approaches to Echmiadzin, no marriage for Nazarian and Satenig is recorded at Paris' Armenian church, nor any funeral for Nazarian.[*]

Back in London, Nerses Gulbenkian married his English cook, Mary Bagge, in 1934 (when Vergin was 18 – the two women loathed each other). Nerses and Mary later moved to Llandudno in Wales, where Mary died in 1945. Gulbenkian died there on 21 May 1957. His obituary in *Sion*, the journal of the Jerusalem Patriarchate, makes no mention of the scandal around Satenig.

> His only son, Boghosik had died unexpectedly and the wound that had caused to the father's heart never healed. We hope God [had made it possible] that he [Nerses] had fallen asleep after being reconciled with his only daughter and the sweet sense of having grandchildren. [...]
>
> Despite having a rather harsh and uncompromising character, Nerses Gulbenkian had been, indeed, a major philanthropist, contributing to charitable organisations, the Armenian Church, as well as to educational and cultural institutions. [...]
>
> In order to perpetuate the memory of Boghosik, he had opened the Boghosian Elementary School in Aleppo, under the auspices of the Diocese. But subsequently, for reasons known only to him, he was forced to close it.[†]

Life in France

Meanwhile in France, Nazarian had by now settled into a quiet life, moving later from Montfermeil to the neighbouring eastern Paris suburb of Le Raincy. He mainly earned his living and supported his

---

[*] Information from Paris baptismal register.
[†] *Sion*, June 1957, p. 167

Abel NAZARIAN

VÉRITÉS HISTORIQUES

SUR

L'ARMÉNIE

PARIS 1953

ՀԱՅ ԵՒ ՀԱՅԱՍՏԱՆ

ՄԵՐ ՀԱՆՐԱԳԻՏԱՐԱՆԻ ՄԷՋ

ԱԲԷԼ ՆԶԱՐԵԱՆ

1954

ԱՐԵԱՑ ԳՐԱԿԱՆՈՒԹԵԱՆ ՑԱՑԿԱՆԻՇՆԵՐԸ

1954

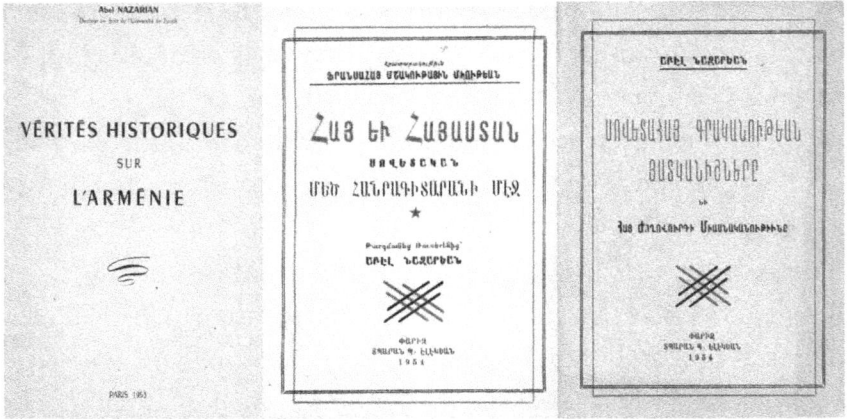

family as a shoemaker. He appears to have deliberately maintained a low public profile. Yet Nazarian continued a sideline as an occasional journalist, his articles and comments appearing intermittently in the Armenian-language press. His writings do not hide his left-wing sympathies.

From 1944, in the dying months of the Nazi German occupation of Paris, Nazarian was connected with the initially hand-written Armenian journal *Joghovourt* (People). Early issues carried the French-language subtitle 'Armenian journal for the struggle against the occupation'. The paper – by now a daily and linked to the Armenian National Front – was among eight left-wing Armenian publications banned by the French authorities. The 7 December 1948 Interior Ministry decree banning *Joghovourt* also banned the Marseille-based weekly *Nor Gyank* (New Life).[*] Nazarian was then connected with the Paris paper *Tsayn Parizi* (Voice of Paris), which seems to have appeared only from January to July 1949.

Later, billing himself as 'Doctor of law of the University of Zurich', Nazarian published in Paris in 1953 a 35-page pamphlet *Vériités historiques sur l'Arménie*, aimed 'principally at young people of

---

[*] Text of decree in Clarisse Lauras, *Les Arméniens à Saint-Etienne: une escale dans un parcours migratoire?* (Publications de l'Université de St Etienne, St Etienne, 2006) p. 66.

Armenian origin who do not understand their maternal language'. He praised 'our dear homeland: Soviet Armenia' and 'the creative force of the genius of the Armenian people, the wisdom of the leaders of Soviet Armenia and the friendship of the great Russian people'. By now in his mid-sixties, he also continued to write in Armenian-language publications, including *Lousaghbyur*, and produced two books in Paris in 1954, one consisting of translations from Russian of entries on Armenia and Armenians in the Soviet Encyclopedia and the other on Soviet Armenian literature. He also conducted studies – for example on education in Armenian among the diaspora – for the Armenian General Benevolent Union in Paris.

The legal status in France of both Abel and Satenig remains unclear. Neither is listed in directories of foreigners gaining French nationality by decree. Nor does any record exist that Satenig became a British subject while she was still living in Britain. As Nerses Gulbenkian became a British subject only in December 1927 – four years after Satenig abandoned London – it appears unlikely she would have. In 1945, as French law required for those reaching the age of 20 whose nationality was in doubt, a declaration was made on behalf of Soussane (possibly by Abel) that she was indeed French.[*]

As for Satenig, in the mid-1950s her surviving British-born child, her daughter Vergin, managed to track down her home in Montmartre in Paris. She knocked at the door of Satenig's down-at-heel flat, hoping to re-establish contact with the mother she had not seen since a couple of days after her seventh birthday, when Satenig and Abel had abruptly departed from London. In a very brief encounter, Satenig told her daughter she loved her, but could not maintain

---

[*] French Interior Ministry file 1945PD001435. The file is probably in the French National Archives but the Interior Ministry has not provided the archives with an index to its many files, making locating this file almost impossible.

Nazarian's home in Le Raincy (Google)

contact. Satenig appeared to be living alone and there was no sign of Abel or their two French-born children.[*]

However, at Nazarian's death on 3 October 1965, his son recorded that he had died at his home in Le Raincy, which he shared with Satenig (given as Satenick Achikian) and Serge (Serob).[†] Nazarian was buried in Le Raincy's municipal cemetery. His plot, No. M 55, has no gravestone or marking. Satenig (given as Satenik Achekian and Nazarian's widow) died at the same Le Raincy home on 25 January 1966. Her death too was registered by Serge, who claimed she had been born in Salmas, Iran, on 30 June 1900, the daughter of Bedros and Marie Manoukian.[‡]

Soussane, who never married and had no children, worked as a school teacher. She died in October 2003. She knew Fr Jirayr Tashjian of the cathedral in Paris, always telling him that she felt God had cursed her family because of her parents' actions. Serob, who was married with

---

[*] Information from Vergin's son, Paul Gulbenkian, January 2018.
[†] Death certificate No. 203, 1965, held at Le Raincy town hall.
[‡] Death certificate No. 12, 1966, held at Le Raincy town hall.

n° 203	Le Trois octobre mil neuf cent soixante-cinq, à quatre heures
Décès de Abel	est décédé, en son domicile, 70 Bis allée de Montfermeil, ABEL,
NAZARIAN	NAZARIAN, né à Salmas, Iran, le quatorze avril mil huit
3 Octobre	cent quatre vingt-dix, sans profession, Fils de Serop NAZARIAN,

et de Soussane GREGORIAN, décédés; - EPOUX de Sate-
rick ACHIKIAN, domiciliée Au Raincy, Seine-et-
Oise, 70 Bis allée de Montfermeil. - Dressé le quatre
Octobre mil neuf cent soixante-cinq, à quatorze heures
trente, sur la déclaration de Serge NAZARIAN, âgé de
trente huit ans, commerçant, domicilié Au Raincy, Mê-
me adresse, fils du défunt, qui, après lecture faite,
a signé avec Nous, Maurice Demorgny, Adjoint au Maire
du Raincy, Officier de l'Etat-Civil par délégation du
Maire ./.

Nazarian's death certificate

children, had his own television repair shop. He died in November
2007. Soussane and Serob both lived in Le Raincy.[*]

Between Faith and Betrayal

The life of Abel Abrahamian – later known as Abel Nazarian –
illustrates the profound entanglement of religion, national identity,
and ideology in the early twentieth century. Born in the Tsarist
periphery, educated in Europe, and eventually implicated in Soviet
politics, his life encapsulates the crises and contradictions that
accompanied the disintegration of empire and the emergence of new
ideological orders. Nazarian's trajectory is situated within the broader
transformations of the Armenian Church in the early Soviet period
and the geopolitical reordering of post-war Europe. Against this
background, his moral ambiguities, personal ambitions and
competing religious and ideological loyalties draw a complex profile
of his character.

---

[*] Information from Fr Jirayr Tashjian, November 2018.

Abel Abrahamian was born in 1888 in Dashburun, a village within the Yerevan *guberniya* of the Tsarist Russian Empire. This region, annexed from Persia in the early nineteenth century, lay at the imperial frontier between Russian administration and the Ottoman sphere. By the late nineteenth century, Tsarist policy in the Caucasus sought to consolidate control while preserving certain privileges of the Armenian Church, whose Holy See at Echmiadzin remained both a religious and national institution.

Abrahamian's education at the Echmiadzin seminary reflected a social pattern characteristic of the time. For many rural Armenian families, seminary education represented an avenue of upward mobility, offering free education and access to modern languages, theology, and classical education otherwise unavailable under the restrictive structures of the *ancien régime*. Ordained as a celibate priest (vardapet) in 1911, Abrahamian's intellectual promise was recognised by the ecclesiastical authorities, who awarded him a scholarship to pursue further studies abroad—part of a broader trend to expose Armenian clerics to European universities.

In 1913, Abrahamian enrolled at Marburg University in Germany, focusing on philosophy and law. The outbreak of World War I, however, placed him in a precarious position as a Russian subject in enemy territory. By 1915, he had transferred to neutral Switzerland, enrolling at the University of Zurich. There he completed his dissertation, *Die Grundlagen des armenischen Kirchenrechts* (The Bases of Armenian Canon Law), and earned his doctorate in 1917. His years in Switzerland coincided with a wave of humanitarian activism surrounding the Armenian Genocide; Abrahamian participated in conferences in Basel and Geneva that raised awareness of the Ottoman massacres and debated the political future of the Armenian nation.

The disintegration of the Ottoman and Russian empires at the close of World War I, coupled with the devastation of the Armenian

Genocide, propelled the Armenian question to the forefront of international diplomacy. When Abrahamian – by then adopting the name Abel Nazarian – arrived in London in 1919, Britain had become a centre of post-war reconstruction and relief advocacy. The short-lived First Republic of Armenia (1918–1920) had emerged from the war's chaos only to fall to Bolshevik control two years later, creating a crisis of representation among exiled Armenian intellectuals.

Nazarian quickly established himself as a dynamic spokesman for Armenian ecclesiastical and national causes. Fluent in several languages and adept in public speaking, he forged close ties with the Church of England, most notably the Archbishop of Canterbury, Randall Davidson. He participated in public platforms such as Armenia and the Settlement, where he appealed for recognition of the Republic of Armenia as 'the nucleus of the Armenian nation'. His position granted him access to diplomatic circles, and in 1920 he served as interpreter for Patriarch Zaven Der Yeghiayan during an audience with King George V – a symbolic encounter that underscored the lingering but cautious British sympathy for the Armenian plight.

Nazarian's involvement in the emerging ecumenical movement further extended his influence. As the sole representative of the Armenian Church at the 1920 World Conference on Faith and Order in Geneva, he was elected to its Continuation Committee, seeking to integrate the Armenian Apostolic tradition into an international Christian dialogue long dominated by Western churches. Simultaneously, he facilitated Calouste Gulbenkian's financial support for the construction of St Sarkis Church in London – an enduring monument of Armenian presence in the capital of the British Empire.

This upward trajectory ended abruptly in 1923 when Nazarian eloped with Satenig Gulbenkian, a married woman and distant relative of his benefactor. The scandal provoked his defrocking and public disgrace, marking the collapse of his clerical and diplomatic career. It also coincided with the definitive Sovietisation of Armenia, closing off the very political avenues he had once championed in Western Europe.

Following his downfall, Nazarian made a startling decision: to return to Armenia, now fully absorbed into the Soviet Union. This move was neither spontaneous nor apolitical. Archival evidence suggests that by late 1923, Soviet security organs had intercepted his correspondence expressing the view that religion led to 'destruction' and offering his services to the 'workers of Armenia'. The Armenian Communist Party soon resolved to 'use the former vardapet for work on disrupting the Armenian clergy'.

Arriving in Yerevan in early 1924, Nazarian became a propagandist within the Soviet anti-religious campaign, writing under the pseudonym Marlen – a contraction of 'Marx–Lenin'. In pamphlets such as *Why I Left* (1924) and *The Armenian Church as a Political and Religious Factor* (1925), he justified his apostasy as a rational political act. The Armenian Church, he claimed, was 'an institution of leadership' aligned with the bourgeoisie and Western imperial interests, 'superfluous and even dangerous' to the Soviet order. These writings aligned closely with the ideological imperatives of the newly-formed League of Atheists (later the League of Militant Atheists), which sought to sever religion's link to national consciousness.

Yet his enthusiasm proved short-lived. By May 1925, disillusioned by the 'material and moral misery' and pervasive censorship of Soviet Armenia, Nazarian sought and obtained permission to leave. That he was able to depart suggests that his usefulness to the regime – as a high-profile defector and propagandist – had secured him privileges unavailable to most citizens.

Nazarian resettled in France, joining a growing Armenian émigré community that included political exiles, intellectuals, and survivors of the genocide. He earned a living as a shoemaker while maintaining intermittent contact with diaspora networks. In 1927, he wrote to Catholicos Gevorg of Echmiadzin, formally retracting his anti-church writings. In his letter, he claimed his earlier propaganda had been produced 'under duress' amid 'the brutalities of Soviet authority'.

Despite this penitence, his subsequent writings suggest continued ideological ambivalence. In 1953, following Stalin's death, he published a pamphlet praising 'our dear homeland: Soviet Armenia' and extolling the 'friendship of the great Russian people'. This expression of admiration, while perhaps sentimental (and possibly encouraged by the Soviet role in defeating Nazi Germany), demonstrates the enduring emotional pull of Soviet Armenia for many exiles who remained alienated from both the Church and Western political structures.

Nazarian lived quietly in France until his death in 1965. Though largely forgotten by contemporaries, his life offers a window into the intellectual and moral crises of an era when traditional forms of faith, nationhood, and authority were repeatedly destabilised by ideological revolution.

Abel Nazarian's life traversed the ideological spectrum of the early twentieth century: from Tsarist-era seminarian to European intellectual, from Anglican interlocutor to Soviet propagandist, and finally to contrite exile. His story reveals not merely a personal drama but a collective pattern of dislocation experienced by Armenian intellectuals navigating the collapse of empire and the rise of ideological modernity.

The shifting loyalties and moral ambiguities that marked Nazarian's career illuminate broader historical tensions within the Armenian diaspora: the struggle to reconcile ecclesiastical identity with secular modernity, the negotiation between Western liberalism and Soviet socialism, and the enduring question of belonging in exile.

Ultimately, his life stands as a cautionary parable of the costs of ambition amid political transformation – a testament to how faith, ambition, and ideology, once fused in pursuit of liberation, could as easily turn into instruments of betrayal.

Questions

Abrahamian/Nazarian leaves a swirl of questions about his extraordinary decade in the 1920s. He was clearly a promising clergyman earning respect from a wide circle of admirers both inside and outside the Armenian Church. In the wake of the genocide and as his homeland plunged ever deeper into isolation and repression, where the Church was soon struggling even to survive, he could have played a key role in continuing to organise, educate and lead its flock in Western Europe and participate in high profile ecumenical bodies. Instead he chose to elope, abandoning his church orders and career, and then even to take the risky decision to return to a Soviet Union which, had he been less lucky, he might never have been able to escape. While he clearly remained sympathetic to the Soviet regime, did he remain an agent of its secret police? No records have yet emerged to confirm this, and the 1930 defector Georgi Agabekov – who revealed that several diaspora Armenian clerics were Soviet agents – makes no mention of him in his published writings. Yet it would seem highly unlikely that Nazarian would have been allowed to leave the Soviet Union without promising to help the regime.

The turbulent times he lived through must have been a contributory factor in his decisions. Europe itself was engulfed in brutal war while he concentrated on his studies. Perhaps more important to him, he could only watch from afar as the Ottoman Empire conducted genocide or forced deportation of almost its entire Armenian population, the Tsarist Empire disintegrated, Armenia emerged as a fragile, poverty-stricken independent state and then felt forced to submit to Bolshevik rule, bringing in its wake a fundamentally new social order. Personally, the religious education he would have experienced at Echmiadzin seminary can only have been a world away from the new theological thinking he would have experienced in Europe, particularly in Marburg and later in Zurich.

Mystery is likely to remain about Abrahamian/Nazarian's motivations, first for abandoning the Church, then working against it and then professing to renounce his earlier opposition. His accounts of his conduct appear not to be entirely truthful. He will remain a controversial figure, a key figure in building London's first Armenian church but who lingers in the folk memory of the city's Armenian community as the 'disgraceful vardapet'.

Abrahamian/Nazarian's Publications

Յ. Ֆ. Հերպարտ եւ իւր մանկավարժական սիստեմը (*J[ohann] F[riedrich] Herbart and his pedagogical system*). Tiflis, 1911 (Armenian)

Հոգեբանութիւն եւ Տրամաբանութիւն (թարգ, գերմ.) (*Psychology and Logic* (Trans. from German)). Vagharshapat, 1913 (Armenian)

Die Grundlagen des armenischen Kirchenrechts (*The Bases of Armenian Canon Law*). Zurich: Leeman and Co., 1917 (German)

The Church and Faith of Armenia. London: The Faith Press, 1920 (English)

Սուրբ Սարգիս եկեղեցի Հայոց Լոնդոնի (*St Sarkis, The Armenian Church, London*). Paris: G. H. Nerses, 1922 (Armenian/English)

Ինչու° Հեռացա (*Why I Left*). Yerevan, 1924 (Armenian)

Հայոց եկեղեցին որպէս քաղաքական յեւ կրոնական գործոն (*The Armenian Church as a political and religious factor*). Yerevan, 1924 (Armenian)

Vérités historiques sur l'Arménie. Paris: Azouz, 1953 (French)

Հայ եւ Հայաստան Սովետական մեծ Հանրագիտարանի մէջ (*Armenia and the Armenians in the* Soviet Encyclopedia). Paris: P. Elekian, 1954 (translation from Russian to Armenian)

Սովետահայ գրականութեան յատկանիշները եւ Հայ ժողովուրդի միասնականութ.jիւնը (*Soviet literature and the characteristics of the people*). Paris: P. Elekian, 1954 (Armenian)

About Abrahamian/Nazarian Publications

Նախկին Վարդապետ Աբել Նազարեանի 'Ինչու Հեռացա' Գրքոյկին Առթիւ. Հրատարակութիւնմ Ս. էջմիածնի Մայր Աթոռոյ Միաբանութեան

(*On the occasion of former Vardapet Abel Nazarian's booklet 'Why I Left'. A publication of the Brotherhood of the Mother See of Holy Echmiadzin*). Paris: Artsakank Parizi Press, 1925 (Armenian).

Also from the Gomidas Institute

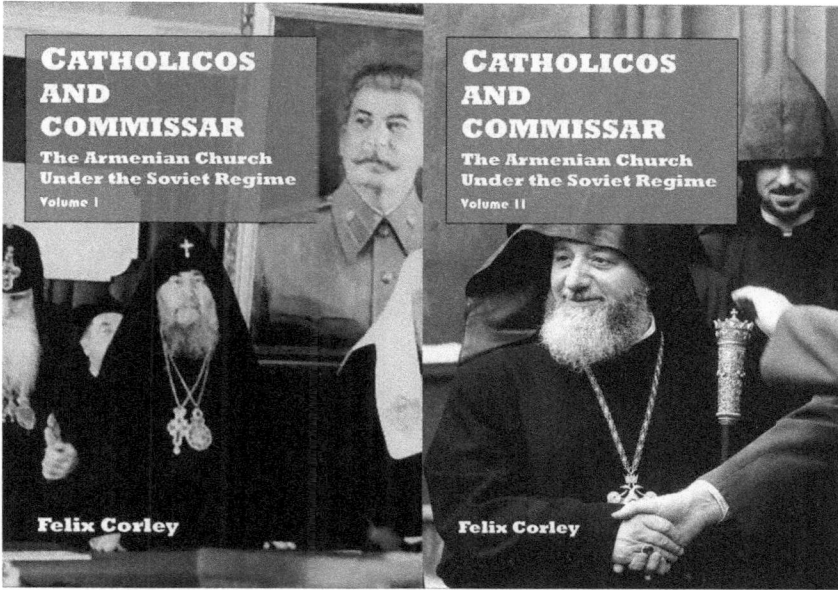

Felix Corley, *CATHOLICOS AND COMMISSAR: The Armenian Church Under the Soviet Regime* (Vol. 1), London: Gomidas Institute, 2025, xlii + 698 pp., maps, ISBN 978-1-909382-84-8.

Felix Corley, *CATHOLICOS AND COMMISSAR: The Armenian Church Under the Soviet Regime* (Vol. 2), London: Gomidas Institute, 2025, ii + 796 pp., ISBN 978-1-909382-85-5.

Gomidas Institute, 42 Blythe Rd., London W14 0HA, England
Email: *info@gomidas.org* * Web: *www.gomidas.org*

www.ingramcontent.com/pod-product-compliance
Lightning Source LLC
Chambersburg PA
CBHW031928080426
42734CB00007B/593